MULTI-FAMILY THERAPY FOR ANOREXIA NERVOSA

Multi-Family Therapy for Anorexia Nervosa is a treatment manual that details an empirically supported and innovative treatment for this disorder.

This book provides a detailed description of the theory and clinical practice of MFT-AN. The treatment draws on the Maudsley Family Therapy for Anorexia Nervosa model as well as integrating other psychological and group frameworks. Part I details the theoretical concepts, MFT-AN structure, content and implementation, including clinically rich and detailed guidance on group facilitation, therapeutic technique and troubleshooting when the group process encounters difficulties. Part II provides step-by-step instructions for the group activities in the initial four-day intensive workshop and for the subsequent follow-up days that occur over a further six to eight months.

The book will serve as a practical guide for both experienced and new clinicians working with children and adolescents with eating disorders and their families, in utilising multi-family therapy in their clinical practice.

Mima Simic is Joint Head at the Maudsley Centre for Child and Adolescent Eating Disorders and a Consultant Child and Adolescent Psychiatrist. She is an internationally recognised expert and trainer in the field of child and adolescent eating disorders.

Julian Baudinet is a Principal Clinical Psychologist with expertise in family therapy and multi-family therapy for adolescents with eating disorders. Alongside his clinical work he is actively involved in treatment and service development, research, teaching and training.

Esther Blessitt is a Principal Systemic Psychotherapist and a team manager in the Maudsley outpatient treatment team. Alongside her clinical work Esther also trains others in the Maudsley eating disorders treatment models.

Andrew Wallis is a Clinical Social Worker and Family Therapist who has worked with adolescents and families for more than 25 years. In 2012 he introduced Multi-Family Therapy for Anorexia Nervosa at Sydney Children's Hospital Network. Andrew provides family therapy training, clinical supervision and consultation to services across Australasia.

Ivan Eisler is Professor of Family Psychology and Family Therapy at King's College London. He is known internationally as a leading developer, researcher and trainer of evidence-based psychotherapies for eating disorders. Ivan has received a number of awards including Academy for Eating Disorders Outstanding Clinician Award, BEAT Lifetime Achievement Award and American Family Therapy Academy Distinguished Contribution to Family Research.

MULTI-FAMILY THERAPY FOR ANOREXIA NERVOSA

A Treatment Manual

Mima Simic, Julian Baudinet, Esther Blessitt, Andrew Wallis and Ivan Eisler

LONDON AND NEW YORK

First published 2022
by Routledge
2 Park Square, Milton Park, Abingdon, Oxon OX14 4RN

and by Routledge
605 Third Avenue, New York, NY 10158

Routledge is an imprint of the Taylor & Francis Group, an informa business

© 2022 Mima Simic, Julian Baudinet, Esther Blessitt, Andrew Wallis and Ivan Eisler

The right of Mima Simic, Julian Baudinet, Esther Blessitt, Andrew Wallis and Ivan Eisler to be identified as authors of this work has been asserted by them in accordance with sections 77 and 78 of the Copyright, Designs and Patents Act 1988.

All rights reserved. No part of this book may be reprinted or reproduced or utilised in any form or by any electronic, mechanical, or other means, now known or hereafter invented, including photocopying and recording, or in any information storage or retrieval system, without permission in writing from the publishers.

Trademark notice: Product or corporate names may be trademarks or registered trademarks, and are used only for identification and explanation without intent to infringe.

British Library Cataloguing-in-Publication Data
A catalogue record for this book is available from the British Library

Library of Congress Cataloging-in-Publication Data
A catalog record has been requested for this book

ISBN: 978-0-367-48233-6 (hbk)
ISBN: 978-0-367-48232-9 (pbk)
ISBN: 978-1-003-03876-4 (ebk)

DOI: 10.4324/9781003038764

Typeset in Zurich
by Newgen Publishing UK

Contents

viii	List of figures
ix	List of tables
x	List of quick reference boxes
xi	List of abbreviations
xii	Acknowledgements
1	**Part I Theory, structure and techniques**
3	**Chapter 1 What is multi-family therapy?**
4	Who is this manual for?
4	Evidence for MFT-AN
4	Effectiveness
5	Treatment acceptability and feasibility
5	Mechanisms of change
7	**Chapter 2 Who can benefit from MFT-AN?**
7	Are all patients and families suitable for MFT-AN?
8	Who should attend MFT-AN?
8	Should siblings attend?
9	**Chapter 3 MFT-AN theoretical concepts**
9	Psychological theories influencing MFT
11	Group theories influencing MFT
13	Eating disorder focused family therapy and MFT-AN
18	**Chapter 4 MFT context and mechanisms of change**
19	How does change occur?
23	**Chapter 5 MFT-AN structure and content**
23	Why are structure and content important?
23	The introductory afternoon
26	The four-day intensive workshop
29	Follow-up days

Contents

32	**Chapter 6 The MFT treating team**
32	MFT treating team members and roles
34	MFT team functioning
34	Pre-MFT preparation
35	When to meet as a team during MFT
35	Content of MFT team meetings
37	Ad hoc and unplanned meetings during MFT
37	Clinical supervision and consultation
38	**Chapter 7 Managing process and group facilitation**
38	Choosing activities
40	Facilitating activities
42	Clinician map to facilitating activities
43	How to develop a new activity
44	Position, proximity and focus
45	The use of self
46	The use of humour and playfulness
47	**Chapter 8 Therapeutic techniques**
47	Interviewing techniques
47	Keeping connected with individuals, individual families and the group as a whole
48	Connecting families with families
48	Connections and differences in the here and now and over time
48	Balancing expertise with lived experience
49	Specific techniques
53	**Chapter 9 MFT meals**
53	Practical aspects of the meals
54	Expectations around mealtimes
54	The role of the MFT team during mealtimes
55	Mealtime clinician map
55	"Foster" family lunch
58	**Chapter 10 Effectively managing and containing the group process**
58	Containing the group and managing affect
58	Managing high affect
60	Steps to managing high affect in the group
60	Managing low affect or engagement
62	Steps to increasing engagement and/or managing low affect in the group
63	When group process is not enough
64	**Chapter 11 MFT troubleshooting and managing risk**
64	Risk management
65	Troubleshooting for other scenarios

Contents

71	**Part II MFT activities**
73	**Chapter 12 How to use activities in MFT-AN**
74	Themes
76	**Chapter 13 Four-day intensive workshop: the activities**
76	Ice breakers / Introduction / Opening activities
78	Activities for increasing motivation and insight into the illness
86	Activities exploring symptom management and mealtimes
94	Activities exploring the impact of the illness on relationships over time
107	Activities exploring looking forward and coping ahead
110	Closing activities for the four-day intensive workshop
111	Mindfulness exercises
113	**Chapter 14 Follow-up days and exercises**
113	Introductory activities for follow-up days
116	Activities targeting motivation, challenging behavioural patterns and their exits, and increasing mutual understanding
120	Activities targeting building relationships, social networks and reflecting on body image
126	Activities targeting facing uncertainty and exploring independence and autonomy
134	Activities exploring the journey through the illness and linking this with the family lifecycle (past, present and future)
137	Activities to end MFT
141	References
146	Appendix I: List of activities by theme
151	Appendix II: List of activities by format
155	Index

List of figures

39	Figure 7.1	MFT clinician toolkit
40	Figure 7.2	Activity decision-making: choosing and carrying it out
42	Figure 7.3	Clinician map to facilitating activities
46	Figure 7.4	Therapist relationships in MFT
59	Figure 10.1	Steps to managing high affect in the group
62	Figure 10.2	Steps to increasing engagement and low level of affect in the group
81	Figure 13.1	Portraits of anorexia: trapped
82	Figure 13.2	Portraits of anorexia: poison
83	Figure 13.3	Portraits of anorexia: two faces
84	Figure 13.4	Pros and cons of anorexia
100	Figure 13.5	Family crest
104	Figure 13.6	Traps and treasures layout
109	Figure 13.7	Family timelines
117	Figure 14.1	Brain scan
119	Figure 14.2	Breaking the chain example
123	Figure 14.3	Care tags
131	Figure 14.4	Safe uncertainty (adapted from: Mason, 1993)
138	Figure 14.5	Recovery recipe

List of tables

11	Table 3.1	Therapeutic factors that influence positive change in group therapy (Yalom, 1995)
13	Table 3.2	The four phases of family therapy for anorexia nervosa (Eisler, et al., 2016b)
18	Table 4.1	Therapeutic factors in the MFT context
24	Table 5.1	Example structure and timing of an MFT day
28	Table 5.2	Example themes for the four-day intensive
31	Table 5.3	Example timing and themes for follow-up days
74	Table 12.1	Structure and timing of MFT days
75	Table 12.2	Example themes and activities for all MFT days
146	Appendix I	List of activities by theme
151	Appendix II	List of activities by format

List of quick reference boxes

24	Quick reference box 5.1	The introductory afternoon
28	Quick reference box 5.2	The four-day intensive workshop
29	Quick reference box 5.3	Change in therapeutic alliance over the course of MFT
30	Quick reference box 5.4	Follow-up days
36	Quick reference box 6.1	Team discussions – key topics
39	Quick reference box 7.1	A guide to choosing MFT activities
56	Quick reference box 9.1	Mealtime clinician map

List of abbreviations

ECG	electrocardiogram
FT-AN	family therapy for anorexia nervosa
MDT	multidisciplinary team
MFT	multi-family therapy
MFT-AN	multi-family therapy for anorexia nervosa

Acknowledgements

Over the more than 20 years that we have been developing multi-family therapy we have collaborated with numerous colleagues and have greatly appreciated the creative thoughts and clinical insights they shared with us, and their ideas are liberally sprinkled throughout the book. Some of this work is published and of course is fully referenced in the book. Much of the inspiration, however, has come from informal sharing of ideas, co-facilitating groups with colleagues or observing and discussing multi-family role plays during training. The people we need to thank especially include past and present members of our team at the Maudsley Centre for Child and Adolescent Eating Disorders. We also want to thank the clinical and research collaborators we have worked with over the years, and colleagues and teams from the UK and many countries around the world that have taken part in our trainings, who had to devise and try out new group activities. There are of course far too many for us to be able to thank individually but a few stand out.

Eia Asen and colleagues at what was then the Marlborough Family Service, the originators of intensive multi-family therapy that inspired this work. Michael Scholz who in parallel with us developed very similar work with his team in Dresden leading to a friendly and very productive rivalry. Our long-term collaboration with Walter Kaye and team at UCSD and in particular Steph Knatz Peck whose five-day Intensive Family Treatment has many similarities with the treatment described in this manual. Andrew and Julian would like to thank Lisa Dawson for her key contribution to the implementation and development of MFT-AN in Sydney.

A special thank you has to go to Tammy Hunt, Anna Konstantellou and Alexander McGookin for helping with finding, checking and rechecking references, proofreading and all their other tireless work in the background.

We also want to thank the hundreds of families who have participated in our multi-family groups, from whom we have learned so much, not only about life with anorexia but also about the strength and resilience that helped them to deal with the illness, which becomes so much more visible when families come together. We want to thank especially the young people who provided the illustrations in the book, which in a different way bring alive their experiences.

Part I
Theory, structure and techniques

Chapter 1: What is multi-family therapy?

Multi-family therapy has a long history going back to the work of Laquer (Laquer et al., 1964) and has been used to treat a range of psychological difficulties including psychosis, mood and anxiety disorders, alcohol and substance misuse as well as school and behavioural problems in children and young people (Gelin et al., 2018). There is also a growing literature on the use of multi-family therapy for eating disorders primarily for adolescent anorexia nervosa (Simic & Eisler, 2015) but also adult anorexia nervosa (Tantillo et al., 2020; Wierenga et al., 2018) and adolescent bulimia nervosa (Stewart et al., 2019). Multi-family therapy for adolescent anorexia nervosa (MFT-AN) was developed as an alternative treatment to inpatient admission for young people who are struggling with anorexia nervosa or other restrictive eating disorders. Since its development in the 1990s (Dare & Eisler, 2000; Scholz & Asen, 2001) it has been used in different formats and range of treatment settings across the world (Gelin et al., 2018; Cook-Darzens et al., 2018). MFT-AN can be delivered in a variety of formats. In this manual we will be describing a specific intensive format, based on the structure and content first developed at the Marlborough Family Day Unit in London (Asen et al., 2001), which has been modified for adolescent anorexia nervosa and has been shown to be efficacious in a randomised controlled trial (Eisler et al., 2016a).

The treatment aims to help improve outcomes for young people with an eating disorder and their families. It brings together families who are struggling with similar difficulties with the aim of increasing knowledge and support, building solidarity to reduce feelings of isolation and changing treatment context by providing multiple sources of information and increasing intensity.

MFT-AN draws on principles from a number of psychological theoretical frameworks, including group psychodynamic therapy, cognitive behavioural, and systemic therapy as well as Maudsley Family Therapy for Anorexia Nervosa (FT-AN). MFT-AN consists of five to eight families (all with a young person suffering with anorexia nervosa, atypical anorexia nervosa or avoidant/restrictive food intake disorder) and a therapeutic team. Ten MFT days are offered over the course of six to eight months and consists of working together as a group for up to 10 full days of treatment. Treatment starts with an introductory afternoon prior to four full consecutive days of therapy. These four consecutive days are then followed by four to six one-day follow-ups. The MFT group is a closed group and the expectation is that families attend both the intensive consecutive days and subsequent one-day follow-up meetings. Follow-up days are initially more frequent, but then their frequency gets spread out, with typically a two-to three-month gap between the last two meetings.

Theory, structure and techniques

Young people and their families who join the MFT group, are expected to be in different phases of treatment, in different stages of their illness with variable levels of motivation towards recovery. Variability has certain advantages and allows families and young people who are early in treatment or who have not made much progress, to witness that change is possible.

This manual is written in two parts. The first part outlines the MFT treatment model including a description of the MFT-AN structure and content, how change is expected to occur, therapeutic techniques, team functioning, and troubleshooting when the group process encounters difficulties. The second part of this manual outlines the structure and content of MFT activities, with detailed instructions, feedback of each activity, and comments we have received from families we treated. The clinical activities described in this manual continue to evolve both as part of our own clinical practice as well through the contribution of a large number of teams that have participated in MFT trainings delivered by the Maudsley Centre for Child and Adolescent Eating Disorders[1]. The activities described in this book are just a selection of activities we use when facilitating MFT-AN.

Who is this manual for?

This manual is written for mental health professionals of varying background and discipline, including but not limited to family therapists, psychologists, social workers, nurses, psychotherapists, psychiatrists and dietitians. MFT can be delivered effectively by clinicians who are not trained family therapists, but it is generally helpful if teams offering MFT include individuals with systemic training. As a minimum, it is important that clinicians planning to facilitate MFT-AN are familiar with the concepts of the Family Therapy for Anorexia Nervosa (FT-AN). FT-AN is an evidence based, four phase treatment that supports the young person and family to return to physical and psychological health by working together in a developmentally sensitive manner. Good understanding, clinical experience and training in the FT-AN model is a prerequisite for anyone planning to offer the MFT-AN intervention. MFT-AN training is also available and is strongly recommended prior to commencing the treatment as it provides a solid grounding in the theory *as well as* the practical elements of running MFT. The training also addresses managing the complex group process, which is unique to MFT and important to consider.

Evidence for MFT-AN

The evidence base for MFT-AN continues to emerge and rests on the shoulders of the 40 plus years of research into family therapy for restrictive eating disorders. Family therapy with an eating disorder focus is now well established as the first-line treatment for children and adolescents (Jewell et al., 2016). A number of recent national treatment guidelines (UK: NICE, 2017; Canada: Couturier et al., 2020; Australia: Hay et al., 2014) recommend family therapy, with the UK and Canadian guidelines including MFT in their recommendations.

Effectiveness

The most recent and largest study of MFT-AN (N=169; Eisler et al., 2016a) is a randomised trial from the UK, which compared MFT-AN with FT-AN. The MFT group also had FT-AN sessions as clinically indicated in between MFT group sessions. The study was conducted in community-based specialist eating disorders services with therapists who were not especially selected for the study but those providing routine care, making this a real-world trial of the model. Results indicated better primary outcomes for the MFT group at

12 months after treatment commenced, with 76% meeting either an intermediate or good outcome using the Morgan Russell criteria (Russell et al., 1987) compared with 58% in the control group. As expected, there were clinically significant improvements for both groups over time with improved weight, eating disorder psychopathology and mood. There were no statistically significant differences on these measures between groups, except the MFT group had gained significantly more weight at 18 months after treatment commenced. There was no difference between the groups in the number of FT-AN sessions over the 12 months of treatment. A second multicentre randomised controlled trial (Carrot et al., 2019) has recently been registered and is aiming to recruit 150 participants comparing MFT and systemic family therapy and will be the first study to compare MFT to a non-eating-disorder-focused family therapy.

A smaller comparison study and a number of case series have also investigated the effectiveness of MFT-AN. Gabel et al. (2014) in Toronto compared the addition of MFT-AN to treatment as usual for 25 patients with a retrospective matched control group from the same service. Treatment as usual consisted of inpatient and outpatient treatment as indicated and also included individual and family therapy. The patients in the MFT group had significantly higher weight than those receiving treatment as usual after 12 months and also had significantly greater improvements in eating disorder psychopathology and mood.

A number of open studies provide additional support for MFT-AN. Salaminiou et al. (2017) reported on 30 patients in the UK who received MFT-AN. There was a significant improvement in weight with 62% in a normal weight range after six months of treatment and two thirds no longer meeting the criteria for a restrictive eating disorder. Improvements in the patient's mood, self-esteem and eating disorder psychopathology were also reported. A case series from Belgium (Gelin et al., 2015) of 82 patients also reported significant weight gain over 12 months of treatment, as well as psychological improvements. Other case series from Denmark (Hollessen et al., 2013); USA (Marzola et al., 2015); Sweden (Dennhag et al., 2019) and Czech Republic (Mehl et al., 2012) also report significant weight gain and/or psychological improvements or improved quality of life after MFT. While there is some variability in the structure and treatment dose in these studies the physical and psychological improvement for patients is consistent.

Treatment acceptability and feasibility

MFT studies consistently report positive parent and patient satisfaction with MFT (Eisler et al., 2016a; Dawson et al., 2018). Qualitative responses reported in these studies reflect planned MFT targets, such as increased understanding of their young person's illness, improved parental capacity, self-efficacy and reduced isolation, although challenges are also reported, and young people do not rate the treatment as highly as their parents (Eisler et al., 2016a). Also notable is MFT's low dropout rate, which varies between reports, but is generally less than 10% (Eisler et al., 2016a; Gelin et al., 2018).

Mechanisms of change

Mechanisms of change in MFT require further research, however, qualitative feedback while limited, seems to match the hypothesised mechanisms. An innovative study (Voriadaki et al., 2015) of one MFT group in the UK tracked participants' experience in a number of ways across the four days of the MFT workshop by making daily ratings of their experience, writing a daily journal and then taking part in separate adolescent and parent focus groups after the four days. Findings from this study indicated that the

Theory, structure and techniques

shared group experience helped both young people and parents to be more insightful and feel less alone. Motivation to recover was enhanced for young people and each family member's position in relation to the other became more defined, allowing young people to become more understanding of their parent's experience and parents increasing in empathy for their offspring's situation and recognising what they needed to do to better help them. Participant feedback also generally followed the expected program goals each day. As one might expect the results were variable at times, with some inconsistency between participants depending on the method of report. Nevertheless, this research and the other qualitative studies provide some preliminary support that the unique context of MFT works in the way it has been theorised.

Note

1 An important part of our MFT training is inviting participating teams to develop new MFT exercises; many of these exercises have become part our own clinical repertoire. There are too many teams to acknowledge individually but we are grateful for the many creative contributions to the evolving practice of MFT.

Chapter 2: Who can benefit from MFT-AN?

Young people can be referred at any phase of treatment, but possibly most benefits are achieved early in treatment for young people who are already engaged enough in outpatient treatment or for young people who are not progressing. For those newer to treatment, intensification of the treatment has the potential to speed up recovery while parents will benefit from receiving extra support from the therapeutic team and other parents in the group. For those who feel stuck in treatment, MFT-AN may provide an opportunity to think about the illness in new ways and to test out new behaviours in a different environment.

Are all patients and families suitable for MFT-AN?
Generally, all young people with restrictive eating disorders can and should be considered for MFT. Some additional thought may be required under the following circumstances:

- Significant comorbidity, particularly severe obsessive-compulsive disorder and/or autism spectrum disorder
- Separated parents/divorced parents/stepfamilies
- Families with significant social care involvement and/or safeguarding risks, such as hostile and/or highly critical family conflicts, or risk of emotional, physical or sexual violence and abuse
- Parents with their own significant mental health difficulties
- Current inpatients

None of these are exclusion criteria per se. In circumstances of severe comorbidity, more pre-MFT preparation might be needed to engage the young person in the process prior to the group, to consider factors such as management of mealtimes, expectation around recovery and the intensity of the MFT process.

Consideration needs to be given in advance of MFT if parents are separated or divorced and in families with historical or current aggression, violence and/or abuse. With divorced parents/stepfamilies, MFT facilitators need to discuss and decide collaboratively with the single-family-therapy therapist and the parents/stepparents, who will attend and when. There is no family constellation that should be excluded on face value; however, more thought may be required around who is participating in what and when. Similarly, attending MFT for parents with severe mental health difficulties and/or significant family issues; families with significant high-risk and current safeguarding issues – especially if this is still under investigation or with no clear safeguarding plan in place. Such factors could be potentially psychologically too overwhelming, and this should be taken into consideration when deciding if the family should attend the group.

Including a family while the young person is an inpatient should be carefully considered, and as a general rule, MFT facilitators should limit the number of families coming from inpatient or day-patient treatment to a maximum of one or two per group. For young people who are inpatients, MFT *should generally be used towards the end of admission but only if parents can make a commitment to supervise meals off the ward in the mornings and/or in the evenings.* For obvious reasons (anorexic competition among young people) young people who require nasogastric refeeding would generally not be included in MFT.

Who should attend MFT-AN?

There is an expectation that eating disorder specialists working with children and their families will have a wide and flexible view of what "family" means to the young people we treat. This flexible view should support the assumption that each family will decide either for themselves or often in discussion with their treating therapist, who is most important to their child in supporting the treatment process. We therefore expect to invite and welcome families to MFT whose composition will often be a mother, father and their child but will also include same-sex couples, parents who no longer live together but have a continuing role in the care of their child, stepparents, grandparents who also have an active role or another member of the extended family who forms part of the child's caring network. If all relevant family members cannot attend, this should not be a reason to exclude a family from MFT; however, expectations should be set that those in a parenting capacity should attend together with the young person whenever possible.

Should siblings attend?

From the very few published studies exploring siblings' experiences of anorexia nervosa in the family (Dimitropoulos et al., 2009; Areemit et al., 2010), we know that siblings' needs can sometimes be overlooked both in therapy and in the family. When the therapeutic focus is on the task of parents supporting a child to overcome anorexia nervosa, siblings may describe feeling that expressing their needs unhelpfully adds an additional burden to family life. They may feel a mixture of concern and worry as well as resentment and anger. Often, they will withdraw or at times may adopt a level of maturity beyond their years and/or attempt to take on a parental role. Unless their needs and thoughts are given space for open expression and validation, there is a risk that we may perpetuate the idea that their needs are less important. Although attending the MFT-AN group may feel daunting to siblings, our experience of including them and prioritising their particular needs for a part of the process has been extremely positive and helpful both to siblings and to their families. Any inclusion in the process of treatment of siblings either in FT-AN or in MFT-AN should be thought about on the basis of the unique circumstances, needs and wishes of the family. Expectations in MFT are that siblings generally attend at least one day during the four-day intensive workshop when the MFT team will facilitate an activity specifically developed for siblings.

Chapter 3: MFT-AN theoretical concepts

MFT draws together a number of psychological, family therapy and group theories and concepts that are outlined below, which together with the context of MFT provide clinicians with an effective approach to conceptualise and support change.

Psychological theories influencing MFT

In the next few paragraphs, we give a brief overview of the psychological concepts developed by Bion, Winnicott, Bowlby, Foulkes, Yalom and more recently by Fonagy and Bateman that have influenced our conceptualisation of MFT. We will start with the concepts that support the formation of the multi-family group as a secure base that creates a powerful context for self-learning, mentalization, emotional expression and affect regulation. All of this is a prerequisite for experimentation with new behaviours that will bring about change on a personal or family level and better management of eating disorder symptoms.

All the theories of psychological processes in human relationships, summarised here, support the notion that human communication has many levels, layers and complexities, but that its essence can be understood as reflecting the process that is formed in the earliest interactions between the infant and primary carers and later reflected in all other relationships that follow.

Attunement and containment

A cornerstone for understanding the essential function of any formative and other key relationships, including relationships in the therapy group situation, is the interaction between the person who provides containment and the person who is contained. Termed by Bion (Bion, 1962; Grienenberger, 2007) the "container" and the "contained". Bion postulated that, well before infants have words, they project unbearable, fearsome, painful, upsetting feelings both linked to their physical and emotional state, into the mother or primary carer allowing the mother/carer to receive this as a communication of their child's state. Mother/carers through empathy, labelling and understanding emotions and thinking, process their child's emotions. In this process, the mother/carers feel emotions themselves, but do not react; they contain the emotions and convey them back to the infant in a more bearable and manageable form, so that the infant can integrate them and over time gradually develop their own capacity to process and regulate their emotions.

Bion, similarly to Winnicott (1953), assumed that an attuned mother/carer can receive and tolerate the projection of the infant's emotional or physical state without denying that they are happening and without becoming overwhelmed. In short, when a hungry and

Theory, structure and techniques

distressed baby cries, the parent/carer who is attuned to their child, knows the baby is not just experiencing hunger, but also a sense of terror and the feeling of being about to fall psychologically apart. If the parent/carer can contain their baby's experiences, they will be able to tolerate the distress and convey this through their words, sounds and physical contact.

In providing containment, the parent, partner, friend, therapist, group members or a group as a whole allow themselves to be affected by the emotional state of the other but are still able to contain and process emotions in a way that emotional states and experiences become more bearable to the others in distress.

Being able to contain emotions of the other person without becoming overwhelmed by the experience is a prerequisite of mentalization (see p. 10) allowing the other person who feels emotionally overwhelmed to perceive their own emotions as being less threatening, as their emotions have not had the same overwhelming effect on people around them.

When the person containing the emotions of another person is unable or refuses to tolerate the distress of the other, a breakdown in the relationship occurs, whether this is a relationship between child and parent, two people, or therapeutic relationship between therapist and patient or therapists and the group.

In MFT there is a matrix of different subgroups working as separate containing units, e.g. each family, MFT team, each subgroup contributing to the whole group containment and cohesion. On occasions when individuals, families or the whole group become overwhelmed by the other person's or other people's emotions, this might make the person, family or families, the MFT team or the whole group feel as though they are falling psychologically apart and consequently they might try to force the anxiety back to the person/people in distress and amplify their anxiety. This recreates a vicious circle corresponding to the relationship between the primary carer and infant when the overwhelmed carer, unable to contain the infant's painful feelings, becomes an untrustworthy object for the infant. In other words, if the family unit becomes uncontained, a parent or parents might project their anxiety onto their child, but if the MFT team, or group as a whole can contain the parents and the family unit, the group is still trusted by all, and the group's process is uninterrupted. However, if the MFT team, or group as a whole, become uncontained, the anxiety in all participants gets amplified, leading to loss of trust in the group as a secure base (Bowlby, 1988), and possible rupture in relationships (attachment) between the MFT team and some or all families in the group follows.

Holding environment
Another conceptualisation that has informed our work is Winnicott's (1953, 1960) concept of the holding environment. For Winnicott the holding environment is the transitional space between people where intimate relationships and creativity occur. He argued that the holding environment facilitates the child's transition to autonomy, and that a similar process is re-enacted and needed in the relationship between therapist and patients. In MFT, the safe and attuned holding environment provides the context of closeness where creative relationships between therapists and the group participants allow families and young people to gradually become less dependent on the therapists and more autonomous and independent.

Mentalization
In recent years the concept of mentalization has influenced our thinking about the MFT process. Mentalization has been defined (Fonagy, 2006) as an imaginative mental ability

to self-reflect and an ability to understand the mental state of others. It enables people to perceive and interpret human behaviour in terms of intentional mental states (needs, desires, goals, beliefs, feelings, purposes and reasons). Being able to mentalize also encompasses being curious and genuinely interested in others, being playful and able to forgive, as well as tolerate that we can only guess what others are thinking but will never know with certainty. Mentalization is a prerequisite for affect regulation including affect regulation of the self. However, capacity to mentalize diminishes under high stress. Once mentalization capacity is "switched off" under high stress, people's thinking becomes inflexible, they hold fixed and concrete views (Long et al., 2020) precluding them from being reflective or responsive to others. In many ways mentalization corresponds and builds on Bion's concept of "container/contained" – the ability to mindfully and with empathy process one's own mental state and cognitions and the mental state of others.

In the development of MFT the aim is that MFT should provide a secure base and safe holding environment that promotes greater independence and emotional development for young people. The MFT team aims to provide containment to the group as a whole, but also to all families and individual participants. The structure and content of the group are carefully designed to be containing. The additional source of containment is that all participants attend the group as a part of their own family. This allows each family to act as a self-contained unit that protects all family members within their own attachment secure base. Initially the group facilitators are very active in bringing in expertise, structure and content, constantly working on enabling mentalizing processes to be sustained and maintained in the group as a whole. The overarching aim is for emotions to be processed to become more manageable and tolerable.

Group theories influencing MFT

Our thinking and theory have been inspired by Yalom's (1995) 11 therapeutic factors that influence positive change in group therapy (see Table 3.1).

Table 3.1 Therapeutic factors that influence positive change in group therapy (Yalom, 1995)

Therapeutic factor	Positive change
Instillation of hope	Creates a feeling of optimism
Universality	Helps group members to realise that they are not alone in their impulses, problems and other issues
Imparting information	Helps group members to acquire knowledge relevant to their specific psychological situation
Altruism	Allows sense of value and significance by helping other group members
Socialising techniques	Promote social development, tolerance, empathy and other interpersonal skills
Corrective recapitulation	Provides for the resolution of family and childhood events within the safety of the group family
Imitative behaviour	Group members learn to adopt the coping strategies and perspectives of other group members
Interpersonal learning	Helps group members to develop supportive interpersonal relationships
Group cohesiveness	Gives group members a sense of acceptance, belonging, value and security
Catharsis	Releases suppressed emotions and promotes healing by disclosing information to group members
Existential factors	Incorporate learning how to just exist as part of something larger than oneself

Theory, structure and techniques

All these factors are an integral part of the therapy of the whole group, in the group and through the group.

In the early phases of MFT, therapists act as experts, imparting information and affirming the knowledge, values and beliefs that underlie and guide their work. Participants' understanding of the therapists' position or "where the therapists are coming from" direct the work of the whole group. Therapists' sharing of their knowledge with the MFT group, combined with openness and curiosity of how this applies to the participants, increases the cohesiveness of the group and promotes exploration of new ideas and interpersonal learning. The introduction of activities and role plays sets up the group as a rehearsal stage for new experiences and new learning. Therapists need to ensure that during MFT new learning is translated and encouraged in real life, so that participants can cope with challenges in a different way. The fact that all families share similar experiences in managing their ill child with anorexia nervosa helps the cohesiveness of the group, it encourages altruism and a wish to help each other. Being surrounded by others "in the same boat" helps with the expression of intense feelings (corresponds to what Yalom referred to as catharsis), and the joint search for new solutions (correcting recapitulation) that contribute to optimism and the instillation of hope.

In MFT, basic group therapy principles are followed, encouraging active participation of all group members (however, see also on p. 25, "right to plead the 5th amendment" in MFT) in a permissive atmosphere that fosters mutual understanding and learning from each other.

Activities and role plays used in MFT to a certain extent resemble psychodrama techniques (Apter, 2003), except that they are much more structured and most of them incorporate experiments and exposure as a core part of the activity. Often when the participants start MFT, they have already developed fixed, rigid patterns in the way they approach mealtimes and family life in general. New experiences and exposure are needed in order to break these rigid patterns.

Group therapist's role

The therapist's initial role is to establish and maintain group functioning. As the group progresses, the therapist's role changes, encouraging the group and participants to become more independent and assume more responsibility for leading the group process and content. As Foulkes (1948) postulated, the group therapist is the instrument of the group, in the service of the group, follows the group's lead and does not forget that the group itself is a therapeutic instrument. This is why the therapist encourages contributions by participants whenever possible.

The intensity of the MFT context does not allow time for therapists to think through all the group processes during each group session. Though all therapeutic interventions in MFT are purposeful, the speed and intensity of group interactions are such that "the conductor could not possibly think it all out, more so as he is to act spontaneously himself if he wants his group to be spontaneous" (Foulkes, 1948, p. 141). In other words, therapists will need during the therapeutic process also to rely on their therapeutic intuition and with "controlled instinct ... must act first but should think about it afterwards" (Foulkes, 1948, p. 141).

This is the reason why regular MFT team meetings have been factored into the MFT daily structure, to allow the team time to discuss and process (mentalize) all the "unfinished business" that emerged for the team or some facilitators during the MFT day (see supervision, p. 37).

Integrating knowledge

Another important premise that our approach to therapy embraces, is that therapists base their intervention on their psychotherapy knowledge and the use of self, but at the same time they are familiar with the recent updates in scientific knowledge concerning anorexia nervosa and use this knowledge in treatment. Therapists follow Ackerman's (1945, p. 713) notion that psychotherapy is "both Art and Science" and that "no amount of art in psychotherapy can excuse an inadequate training in psychopathology. The art in psychotherapy must be made to serve the science and not vice versa".

Eating disorder focused family therapy and MFT-AN

MFT-AN integrates the more general concepts of MFT (Asen & Scholtz, 2010; Simic & Eisler, 2015) with the theoretical concepts of single-family therapy for anorexia nervosa (FT-AN) (Eisler, et al., 2015; Blessitt, et al., 2020; Simic & Eisler, 2018). The FT-AN therapy model has been developed, modified and manualised (Eisler, et al., 2016b) over the years by the team at the Maudsley Centre for Child and Adolescent Eating Disorders service in London, UK.

The FT-AN therapy model aims to strengthen a sense of parental self-efficacy and maximise family resources in overcoming their child's anorexia nervosa. The young person's family is perceived as a protective factor (not a cause of the illness) and is a part of the solution in the management of the young person's eating disorder symptoms. FT-AN follows four phases of treatment, for details see Table 3.2 and a very brief descriptions of the main concepts and interventions characterising each of these phases.

Phase 1 *Engagement and development of the therapeutic alliance with the patient and her/his family*

In FT-AN, it is expected that the initial assessment will be provided by a multidisciplinary team (MDT), which provides the context of engaging the family in treatment. A key part of the initial assessment is a physical examination of the patient (including weight, height, vital signs, baseline blood tests, ECG etc.). The physical examination serves a dual-purpose, a) assessing the level of medical risk and b) communicating to the family the multidisciplinary expertise of the team as a whole, both functions supporting the establishment of a secure base for treatment. From the outset the assessing team, directly or indirectly, states their position that the treatment that follows is a collaborative treatment *with the family* and not the treatment *of the family*. Starting from the assessment, the MDT acts from a position of expertise in the eating disorder, introducing psychoeducation focused on the eating disorder (predisposing factors and neurobiology of anorexia nervosa) and simultaneously conveying the MDT's understanding of what the young person and their family are going through (the impact of anorexia nervosa on young person and

Table 3.2 **The four phases of family therapy for anorexia nervosa (Eisler, et al., 2016b)**

Phase I	Engagement and development of the therapeutic alliance with the patient and their family
Phase 2	Helping families to manage the eating disorder and the young person's return to physical health
Phase 3	Helping the young person to re-establish independent eating as well as supporting their greater independence and autonomy. Exploring issues of individual and family life cycle post anorexia nervosa
Phase 4	Ending treatment and discussion of future plans and discharge

Theory, structure and techniques

family). Understanding and validation of the family's current shared suffering and difficulties can help build the development of trust between the assessment/treatment team and family, which in turn promotes the development of the therapeutic alliance and deepens the engagement with the treatment team.

Psychoeducation on eating disorder consists of a number of components:

Temperament and personality traits as risk factors for anorexia nervosa

Scientific knowledge accumulated in recent decades has indicated a number of temperament and personality traits that act as predisposing factors for the development of anorexia nervosa (Kaye, et al., 2013). This includes anxious personality traits ("persistent or constant worriers"), often accompanied with a sensitivity to other people's feedback, especially when the feedback is perceived as critical (Solmi et al., 2019). The high threat-sensitivity linked with the overanxious personality traits leads to propensity to perceive ambiguous cues as threatening to trigger anxiety further (Cardi et al., 2013). At the same time, people predisposed to developing anorexia nervosa tend to suppress the expression of their negative emotions (Lang, et al., 2016) because they believe that this will be seen as a sign of weakness and vulnerability (Hambrook et al., 2011). Maladaptive perfectionism (Halmi et al., 2000) has also been identified meaning that young people who develop anorexia nervosa may also have exceptionally high and inflexible standards for themselves leading to an overwhelming fear of making mistakes and negative social comparison with others. High focus on details (Lopez et al., 2008) can result in lacking a bigger picture perception when thinking about the difficulties they may encounter in their lives. Intolerance of uncertainty (Frank et al., 2012) leading to inflexibility and need to control, coupled with determination and persistence, may all contribute to the development and maintenance of anorexia nervosa (Cassin and von Ranson, 2005).

Neurobiology of anorexia nervosa and the starved brain

Many symptoms seen in anorexia nervosa are the result of an interplay between the predispositions and body/brain starvation that is the consequence of severe food restriction. Most frequent triggers for food restriction in young people, are the negative events that can occur during adolescence. Some potential triggers observed in clinical practice include bullying, cyberbullying, being excluded from a peer group, negative comments from peers, family or others about the young person's shape and weight, or physical illness in a parent. These experiences will commonly lead to feeling miserable, lonely or to having low self-esteem. A conscious decision to restrict food is usually an attempt to feel better, healthier, more fit, or more attractive. Initially weight loss can be inadvertently reinforced by positive comments from others. However, with more significant weight loss, there are changes in the brain and body neurobiology (Frank et al., 2019). Changes in gut hormones, sexual hormones and other brain hormones will result in changes in behaviours and cognitions. Starvation is also associated with changes in brain neurotransmitters that will lead to functional and structural brain changes found in neuroimaging studies (Frank et al., 2019). Complex brain-body changes triggered by starvation, have as a consequence that food is no longer, a reward, on the contrary, food restriction that temporarily relieves anxiety becomes the reward. The more anxious the person is, the stronger the drive to restrict food to temporarily reduce anxiety. Eating is often followed by feelings of guilt. Guilt after eating may be in part due to the young person's perfectionistic tendencies, meaning that they perceive eating adequate amounts of food to gain weight as failing in the personal goal they have set for themselves to restrict food intake and lose weight. Raised anxiety, changes in perception of hunger and own body, further reinforce the drive for thinness and body image dissatisfaction. All of this sets up the vicious cycle of food restriction in anorexia nervosa and the longer it lasts the more physical consequences are going to follow at the brain-body axis. In the full-blown anorexia nervosa, all the body systems are involved and altered and some of the abnormalities may result in long-term consequences, e.g. irreversibly low bone density.

Setting up shared goals
Engagement of the whole family in treatment and establishment of a family therapeutic alliance promotes the development of a shared narrative between the therapeutic team and the family about the nature of the illness that helps in agreeing shared goals for treatment. The initial goals of treatment are to secure physical safety and adequate and regular weight gain. Achieving these goals will be a basis for the next phases of treatment. In order for this to be achieved the therapist explains that the young person will be weighed at the beginning of each session, and a meal plan might be offered if the family considers this to be useful. The importance of early behavioural change around eating and nutrition is emphasised as well as the crucial role that parents have in managing their child's eating disorder symptoms and eating.

Parental meal supervision as an act of parental care
Acknowledging and validating the anxiety that has been triggered by the presence of anorexia nervosa can help in the mobilisation of family resources, but most importantly the therapist clearly defines and describes the parental role in managing their child's eating as an act of care and love. The psychoeducation about the neurobiology of anorexia nervosa and the physical and psychological effects of starvation aim to validate the child's experiences of being tormented by their eating disorder cognitions while emphasising that these are an unavoidable consequence of the illness. The therapeutic team's confidence that recovery from anorexia nervosa is achievable, helps to contain parental anxiety and accept the inevitable distress of their child in the short term. The best care that parents can offer is to support their child to eat and gain weight, as this is an essential and necessary precondition for the brain-body recovery from starvation.

Externalisation
Parents are often confused with the behavioural changes of their child during the illness. Externalisation or separating cognitions, behaviours or physical consequences linked with anorexia nervosa from the personality of their child often helps parents and young people to gain a different perspective on the situation they are in. By the time the young person and their family come to treatment, family life and organisation has already been severely impacted by the illness, with feelings of distress, worry, frustration, anger, helplessness and hopelessness dominating the family's emotional climate. Being able to understand

Theory, structure and techniques

the symptoms of anorexia nervosa as symptoms of an illness and distinct from the personality of the child can help parents to reduce emotional reactivity to the behavioural and cognitive changes of their child.

Formulation

Developing a formulation is an important component of treatment. Information gathering for the collaborative systemic formulation starts at assessment and is revisited throughout treatment. The formulation is developed collaboratively with the family establishing the base for a shared roadmap towards recovery. The formulation helps the therapist to increase understanding of the family system, clarify hypotheses and questions they have around the family reorganisation around anorexia nervosa symptoms and symptom management. The formulation orients therapist in prioritising which issues to focus on and how to plan treatment and select specific interventions. The formulation is always linked to theory and is a base for determining criteria for successful outcome (Butler, 1998).

Phase 2 *Supporting/helping families to manage the eating disorder and enable the young person's return to physical health*

Phases one and two of treatment overlap and all interventions that started in phase one, e.g. defining the meaning of parental meal supervision as an act of parental care, psychoeducation, externalisation and developing collaborative systemic formulation, will continue in phase two. The therapist supports and contains parental anxieties while encouraging parents to accept and validate their child's distress linked with food and eating. Different strategies are used including coaching parents in ways how they can reduce and contain their child's anxiety during mealtimes. Parental reactions during mealtimes are explored, and parents are helped to establish clear and predictable rules around meals and encouraged to appropriately use distractions while remaining firm but compassionate to their child's distress. The therapist continues to explore the impact of anorexia nervosa on family relationships and focuses on increasing engagement with the young person ensuring that the young person's voice is heard in the session and outside of the session. The specific role of each parent during mealtimes is explored including ways that they can support each other by giving the other time for breaks, but also working as a team. It is expected that during this phase the young person will accustom to regular eating under parental supervision with steady weight gain that will result in physical recovery. Usually by the end of this phase parents regain a sense of hope and the young person is feeling better understood, their mood has improved, and they have accepted (though grudgingly) the need for weight gain.

Phase 3 *Helping the young person to re-establish independent eating as well as supporting her/his greater independence and autonomy. Exploring issues of individual and family life cycle post anorexia nervosa.*

This phase is characterised by handing back to the young person the responsibility for food choice, its amounts and eating and their life in general. Focus of the therapy is on improving tolerance to uncertainty, self-acceptance and taking on the responsibility for own actions. Shared and non-shared temperament and personality traits that once were the risk factor for development of anorexia nervosa are explored with a new lens. Novel ways of managing these vulnerabilities and emotions that they bring are encouraged, which do not involve the restriction of food as a way of abating the young person's anxiety. The young person and the whole family are supported to discover or rediscover having fun together and each of them as a separate individual. Focus of the therapy is on reviewing the family relationships and how the whole family and each person separately can move on in their life cycle.

This phase also entails a change in therapeutic relationship between the family and the therapist, with the therapist stepping back and taking a less central role, in other words relinquishing an active expert role and assuming a more non-directive role encouraging family members to find their own solutions to the problems they are facing in their everyday life.

Phase 4 *Ending treatment and discussion of future plans and discharge*
It is important that the ending or therapeutic relationship is explored in a timely manner and that enough time is dedicated to reviewing the family journey through treatment. One of the goals in this phase of treatment is to discuss issues of responsibility for management of any remaining or future difficulties including ways of seeking help if needed. Relapse prevention and exploring current and future family life without anorexia nervosa are an integral part of the treatment ending.

Chapter 4: MFT context and mechanisms of change

MFT-AN interventions are aimed at intensifying and modifying FT-AN through three main mechanisms; changing the treatment context and intensity, creating space to address multiple treatment targets simultaneously, and bringing people together to reduce isolation, stigmatisation and opportunities for families to learn from each other. By adding in these elements to FT-AN, young people and families are able to create new understandings, new meanings and to experiment with new behaviours in a way that cannot be accessed through single family therapy. The overarching goal of MFT-AN is to enhance the speed of change and recovery from anorexia nervosa. The collaborative environment of MFT is also an effective way of reducing the potential for the development of deleterious staff/patient relationships that can otherwise seriously hamper the progress of treatment (Asen & Scholz, 2010).

Some ways in which the multi-family group context might facilitate change include:

Table 4.1 Therapeutic factors in the MFT context

Instillation of hope	Gaining hope from observing what others have tried/achieved
Psychoeducation	Gaining new insights into the nature of AN and the underpinning neurobiology
Creating a containing, safe context for learning	Feeling understood and validated as an individual
Experience of communality	Gaining a sense of having a shared problem with other families
Overcoming isolation and stigmatisation	Gaining a sense of belonging to a group
Learning from observing others	Gaining insight into how things can be done differently
Learning from being observed by others	Revealing oneself to others and getting their reactions
Learning from other's perception of own family	Openness to hear and learn from the feedback from others
Forgiveness	Understanding the actions of others and accepting them as they are
Gaining new perspectives	Perceiving problems in a new light
Taking risks in trying new behaviours	Feeling secure to try something new
Taking risks in sharing emotions and vulnerabilities	Feeling secure to express vulnerable emotions
Group cohesiveness	Identifying with the group both individually and as a family
Humour and playfulness	Enjoying having fun together

MFT context and mechanisms of change

How does change occur?

Multiple sources of input

The treatment context of MFT is vastly different to FT-AN and most other therapeutic interventions, including most group-based interventions. Having a combination of patients, family members, carers and professionals in the room at any one time offers a unique opportunity for multiple sources of knowledge and experience to be introduced into an individual family's treatment. This sharing of "insider knowledge" is important to the process of MFT as it allows for people to be the provider and recipient of information from multiple sources. This can be a powerful component of treatment as the same input provided by one person (e.g. a professional) may be heard and taken on to varying degrees and in different ways as that provided by another person with different and more personal experiences (e.g. a parent or young person). The intensive MFT groups described here also provide multiple learning opportunities, e.g. listening to and observing other families, trying out new behaviours in a supportive and safe environment, taking part in a wide range of verbal and non-verbal activities and reflecting on the experience and process of these activities.

Each member of the group, regardless of their role in the family or team, brings their own individual strengths, skills, resources and experiences. One of the most important elements of the structure and process of MFT is that it allows family members to move in and out of many different roles, such as that of the patient, expert, witness, coach or carer. This process is powerful as it creates the opportunity for learning and relearning of old and new ideas related to the illness and to family life. Allowing participants to move out of one particular role and into another, together with new experiences and their interpretation, creates new knowledge, meaning, insight and hope. Furthermore, the same dilemmas people may experience within themselves or their family will likely be played out in various ways with others during MFT, allowing for reflection in a way that is not possible outside of this context. All families typically develop specific patterns of interaction that are a reflection of their relationships. In families where specific problems have developed, such as an eating disorder, these often become more restricted and difficult to change and may take on both a protective role as well becoming part of the maintaining pattern of the eating disorder (Eisler, 2005). Interacting with other families in the MFT allows families to become more aware of and question their specific ways of coping and allows new patterns to emerge.

Just as people in the group take on different roles, they are also at different phases in treatment and recovery. This allows young people and families the opportunity to think about and see the way the illness, individuals and families may change over time. It is a common experience of young people and their families to become very narrow in their time focus when in the throes of the illness. People describe struggling to think beyond the here and now, beyond the hour or day ahead. By seeing young people and families at different stages, people begin to move in and out of how things may shift over time and how someone's needs may differ depending on the stage of recovery, stage of adolescence and their family life cycle.

Most importantly, the core of the MFT process is to allow many opportunities for learning through doing, rather than just talking. MFT participants often report that the MFT context helped them to experience or communicate things that they have struggled with

Theory, structure and techniques

in words. It also provides real time information for clinicians about how families interact as well as offering practical, *in vivo*, support.

What does it look like?
As an MFT clinician it will be important to ensure that the group members are interacting with one another and able to sustain mentalization throughout the group process. Facilitators need to keep an eye on comments, behaviours and shifts in affect as signs of new learning and understanding. Change will take place at many levels and may be in some instances very obvious and at other times quite subtle and easily missed. This could be as simple as a sibling or parent's voice being softer (kinder) or more patient, where they had previously come across as annoyed, angry or frustrated. It could also be bigger, more obvious gestures like an apology after a moment of insight, or one member of a family saying to another "I had no idea how hard it was for you". Indicators of change will not always be verbal. Following on from experiential tasks, many participants will have a new appreciation for the struggle that others are going through, not just themselves. This may be expressed with increased warmth or simply being more present, patient and available.

Increased intensity and the broadening of treatment scope
The MFT-AN structure is specifically designed to provide intensive support to young people and families early in treatment. The initial four days are provided over consecutive days, each lasting six hours. Thereafter, four to six follow-up days are provided, each of which is also six hours in length. Initially follow-up days are spaced close to one another, usually after one or two weeks, to facilitate group engagement. Thereafter follow-up days are increasingly spaced out to six to eight weeks as participants gain confidence and move towards independence individually and as a family.

The intensity of treatment is purposeful in that it matches the needs of the families as they progress along the path to recovery, and it parallels the structure of FT-AN. The increased intensity also allows for treatment targets to be broadened to ensure that the main tasks of FT-AN can be discussed while simultaneously having enough time to address other issues that may be co-occurring, such as, additional family difficulties, identity and lifecycle issues, managing comorbidities or working with peer/social concerns, which may not have been addressed due to time constraints.

The structure has also been described as creating a "hot house" environment (Asen & Scholz, 2010). The experience of attending a therapeutic group for six hours per day can feel emotionally charged, but equally emotionally safe and containing. This "hot house" allows people to move beyond their usual responses and defences in order to try out new behaviours, experience and express emotions and see things from multiple perspectives.

What does it look like?
The MFT pace and intensity is a key part of the treatment. The facilitators should take note of participants' emotional energy levels as well as how defensive they appear. They should observe when someone responds to a situation in a way that is not the way they normally would. This might include demonstrating firmness or flexibility where it was not previously the case. It might include responding to a situation with compassion rather than criticism. When the pace is most effective, typically participants will be able to reflect,

leading to new realisations, such as that there is an urgency for immediate change in behaviours, patterns or attitudes, rather than waiting to see what will happen. Reflection can lead to new insights, e.g. that they need to let go of anxiety that might be hindering progress.

Solidarity, reduced isolation and building a community

One of the most common experiences reported by people with eating disorders and their families is that they feel isolated by the experience because they feel that their experience is so different and at odds to the experiences of everyone around them. People often speak about feeling as though even those who are closest to them don't quite understand what they are going through, which often leads to having less access to support. The most common feedback from those who attend MFT is that meeting others in a similar position to them is incredibly powerful, moving and relieving. While this does not necessarily change anything practically, the solidarity with others has been almost unanimously reported as one of the most helpful elements of the MFT process.

What does it look like?

Over the course of treatment, all participants and staff will become much more familiar and comfortable with each other. The first day of MFT is often filled with anxiety for all participants (including therapists), but fairly quickly a richness of interactions between families, both during treatment days as well as between MFT days, gets developed. Facilitators should watch out for parents turning to other parents for advice, or young people offering a hug, words of encouragement or suggesting to play a game, as signs that solidarity is building. Parents will often create relationships outside the group and share advice, tips, encouragement and support. While not necessarily explicitly instructed, this is encouraged if this contact is supportive and constructive.

Experimenting with new ways of doing things

A key component of MFT is providing the opportunity and support to engage in new behaviours. The change elements outlined (see Table 4.1) create a foundation of a secure base for trying new ways of doing things in the group. New behaviours are encouraged in all aspects of the treatment through the formal activities, supported mealtimes, and less formal interactions in the "corridor". Facilitators should be mindful to recognise opportunities to invite participants to do new things remembering that *in vivo* opportunities are likely to lead to greater change than delaying a change to another time. These changes can then be strengthened by providing further opportunities inside and outside the group times. Of course, reported and *in vivo* changes are also being observed by other families and this should spur others on to try something new.

What does it look like?

The main factors for the facilitators to monitor are the level of engagement, mentalizing capacity and emotion in the room and how these impact upon people's behaviour and their interaction with others. Behaviour, however small, is the most obvious sign of change that facilitators should be on the lookout for. This might include someone doing something different around mealtimes, such as a parent providing a more suitable meal or snack, remaining firm when that had previously been difficult, or for a young person to eat with less resistance or arguing. Behaviour change may often, however, not be directly

Theory, structure and techniques

related to mealtimes and may therefore appear less significant at face value. This may include things like a parent putting their arm around a child or partner for comfort, a family arriving on time when they have previously been consistently late, a normally distant/distracted/avoidant parent being more present and consistent during activities/meals, a moment of tenderness between two people where there is usually tension, or a shift when a family previously sitting apart choose to sit together during activities.

While not necessarily large changes, these are all clues that there has been a shift in emotion within an individual or family unit and is often associated with new learning/insight and increased mentalizing capacity. A good example of this is during the family sculpt activity (see p. 94) of a young person moving across the room and giving her father a hug. A small act that would be easy to miss for the facilitator if focusing on the task at hand, but crucially important as a marker of change for that family where there had been strong feelings of resentment and feeling misunderstood. Through the family sculpt task the young person was able to see her family dynamic in new ways, which softened the tension and promoted closeness.

Changes in engagement and accompanied affect created during activities may be even more subtle but are equally important to notice and amplify where possible. These will also be markers of a change in thinking, capacity to mentalize, a shift in understanding, or gaining a new insight. Clues to facilitators will be any changes in demeanour/body posture of participants or in emotion within the therapist themselves. For example, facilitators might just notice that someone who usually presents as agitated is finding a moment of stillness, or perhaps someone who appears quite passive becomes animated and energised. This is usually (although not always) coupled with a reflective comment, which can be useful to highlight if appropriate. A small example of this was noticing that a mother, who had previously been very quiet and made a point of sitting across the room from the facilitators at all times, decided to sit next to the facilitators during a task. Similarly, a father who is silent during an activity, when he is usually quite vocal, is a moment to notice, understand and possibly attend to if appropriate.

Chapter 5: MFT-AN structure and content

This chapter outlines the structure (what each day looks like/what happens when) and content (what gets talked about) in MFT-AN. This includes the timing and format of MFT days, the content discussed and aspects of the physical environment to consider. The third component, group process, is described in Chapter 7. Content, structure and process all need to be carefully considered to effectively facilitate MFT-AN.

Why are structure and content important?

Having a clear structure and planned content for all MFT days serves multiple important functions. Together these help to a) contain the group and create a secure base for treatment, b) ensure treatment is targeted and matches participants' goals, and c) reduce anxiety in the MFT team.

Predictability of the MFT structure helps to simultaneously reduce and contain anxiety and improve mentalizing capacity of the families attending MFT and the MFT team delivering the treatment. The four-day intensive workshop and the follow-up days have the same structure, intermixing mealtimes with activities within a consistent and predictable timetable (see Table 5.1). The MFT structure is also flexible enough to support different aims, progression, process and pace of treatment as needed.

MFT structure

The main MFT-AN structure consists of three treatment parts; the introductory afternoon, the four-day intensive workshop and four to six single follow-up days spaced over a six-month period. Each part is essential for the treatment and serves an important function. Each part also has its own internal structure. The three parts are aimed at supporting families to transition from engaging, to preparing them for change, offering intensive support in order to try out new things, and then tapering off clinician input, handing back responsibility to families and preparing for endings. The introductory evening and the four-day intensive workshop fit most closely with phase I and phase II of FT-AN. The follow-up days are then designed to start targeting more phase III and phase IV issues.

The introductory afternoon

The MFT team meets all the families who will attend the MFT for the first time at the introductory afternoon. The aim of the introductory afternoon is to engage all participants, to orient them to treatment and to provide psychoeducation about anorexia nervosa. The basic structure of the introductory afternoon consists of an introduction to the therapy

Theory, structure and techniques

Table 5.1 **Example structure and timing of an MFT day**

Time	Task
10:00–11:00	Intro/Opening activity
11:00–11:30	Snack + Break
11:30–13:00	Activity
13:00–13:30	Lunch
13:30–14:00	Break
14:00–15:00	Activity
15:00–15:30	Snack + Break
15:30–16:00	Closing activity

Quick Reference Box 5.1 **The introductory afternoon**

Quick Reference Box: The introductory afternoon	
Aims	• Orient young people and families to treatment • Engage young people and families and reduce anxiety about the group • Provide psychoeducation about anorexia nervosa and associated physical and psychological difficulties

Timing and structure	• 90 min.
	• Approximate timings:
	  - 20 min. Introduction to the treatment, what to expect and the team
	  - 20 min. Medical presentation
	  - 30 min. Meeting a graduate family
	  - 20 min. Discussion and closing time with the whole group
	• Usually occurs Thursday/Friday afternoon/evening, the week before the group starts

Content	• Mini-lectures from MFT team orienting to treatment, discussing structure of the following four days, what will happen at mealtimes, pleading the fifth amendment, and any other practical issues • Mini-lecture from medical professional about the physical and psychological effects of starvation and AN • MFT families meet a MFT "graduate" family
Process	• Initially didactic with a "lecture format" to reduce anxiety and allow participants to settle • Informal and relatively unstructured interaction with "graduate family" • Provide some opportunity to have tea and coffee and to mingle with others at the end

team and treatment, medical talk, and "meet the graduate family" (see Quick Reference Box 5.1).

The introductory afternoon is a relatively formal session, held for 90 minutes on one afternoon in the week prior to MFT commencing. Often this session is held on the Friday afternoon before a group starts the following Monday or Tuesday. The initial formality of the setting is achieved through setting up the seating like a classroom with the therapy team sitting or standing in a row facing the MFT participants.

In the first part of the introductory afternoon, once the team has introduced themselves, outlined the MFT-AN structure of the four-day intensive workshop and follow-up days, the rationale for treatment and any other housekeeping items are addressed. Mealtimes are often a source of high anxiety for the young people and families, so it is important to outline what to expect to try and reduce some of this anxiety. It is reiterated that joint meals are as much a part of treatment as the other components of MFT-AN and that there is an expectation that everyone will finish all meals with support as needed. Prior to MFT, the young person has been assessed with her/his family, and in most cases they have already engaged in the single FT-AN, meaning expectations around meals should already have been put in place. Parents are instructed to bring food for two snacks and lunch for all members of their family for every day of MFT. It should be reiterated that parents are expected to bring food for their child in accordance with their current physical health and weight gain/maintenance needs.

In this initial part of the introductory afternoon, we also introduce the metaphor of "pleading the fifth amendment".[1] Facilitators introduce the idea that the right to refuse to answer questions or take part in a particular activity (simply by saying "I plead the fifth") is helpful for everyone and applies as much to parents as the young people. This intervention should be coupled with an explanation that participants in MFT learn in different ways from the group. Some learn by listening to others, some by observing, some by talking and some by doing, and the way people learn often also changes over time over the course of the group. Each of these ways of learning is valid and useful.

Introducing the "right to plead the fifth amendment" has three related aims. First, it can help participants feel safe in the group while enabling therapists to ask important and difficult questions. The hope behind this is that it can reduce anxiety about being forced to speak in a large group when it may not feel safe or appropriate. Second, it emphasises that each individual has the right and responsibility to decide what personal information they want to share with the group and when they do it. Third, it offers an alternative meaning to some of the behaviours that are likely to be observed in the group (particularly early on) when young people, and sometimes parents, are reluctant to take an active part in activities. This may allow parents, who are anxious that if their daughter/son does not immediately take an active part in the group they will not benefit from the treatment, to give the young person space to join more actively when they are ready. We have observed many instances of participants who have appeared quite passive and unengaged in the early phases of a MFT group, who have then made quite dramatic changes on days three or four.

Families will be reminded of their "right to plead the fifth amendment" at the beginning of the first MFT day in order to help them with any heightened anxiety they might experience due to a threat of self-exposure in the group situation. In our experience, the "fifth" is rarely, if ever, invoked by families. Therapists, however, can find it liberates them to be curious with families. If a therapist feels that a question they are about to ask might be difficult they might preface it by saying "this may be a difficult question and you may want to plead the fifth", or if they get the somewhat stereotypical answer "I don't know" it can be helpful to follow that up with "I'm not sure if this is your way of pleading the fifth because you don't want to say or if you really don't know the answer".

After the introductions, housekeeping and a broad description of the week ahead, a medical talk is given that outlines:

- the temperament and personality traits' predispositions that place young people at risk to develop anorexia nervosa, (see Psychoeducation FT-AN, p. 14)
- the neurobiology of physical and psychological effects of starvation leading to anorexia nervosa (see Psychoeducation FT-AN, p. 14)
- the necessity of restoration of nutritional health to enable recovery
- the positive long-term prognosis when families are supported to bring about such change

Theory, structure and techniques

The talk aims to validate parental efforts and emphasise the seriousness of the illness. The reason behind this is to try and mobilise parents to try out new things and to provide them with a rationale if they need to encourage their daughter or son to attend should there be some ambivalence. The talk should be realistic about the physical and psychological risks of long-term illness but should also offer hope for recovery.

In the second part of the afternoon the young people and their families are given an opportunity to talk to a "graduate family" who has previously completed the MFT and is either in the final phase of treatment or has recently completed it. After the "graduate family" is introduced to the MFT group, young people and parents are separated (if both parents from a "graduate family" attend, then mothers and fathers are also separated) and they meet with their respective graduate family "counterparts". The "graduate" family members then share their experiences of attending MFT and talk about the stepping stones of their journey through treatment towards recovery. If siblings have come along, we suggest they stay in a parent group, to minimise the potential anxiety of being separated so early on from the parent/s.

It is not uncommon that hope and enthusiasm can be ignited when MFT families listen to the experiences of the family who were once in their "shoes". Witnessing positive attitudes from the recovered young person can be enormously helpful for the new MFT participant parents and young people (although young people may remain ambivalent at this stage). Quote from a parent's feedback on the impact of the introductory afternoon on their family:

Meeting with a 'graduate family' in the week before we began, gave us hope before it even started. That family said that they too hadn't known what to expect but that their daughter had benefited. I think the term family therapy was a bit off putting as you worry that a judgment will be made on you, but that turned out not to be the case. It is reassuring knowing how other families are dealing with the situation and definitely good to feel you have experts that can give advice and their thoughts.

Sometimes family members can be reluctant to fully commit to attending MFT. They may feel uncomfortable in large groups or have had a difficult previous experience with other groups. On occasion families are asked to attend the introductory afternoon, get more information and decide on their MFT attendance following the introductory afternoon. With few exceptions, families after attending the introductory afternoon decide to come to the following four-day intensive workshop. If reluctance comes only from the young person with an eating disorder, parents are encouraged to firmly support the young person to attend treatment, similarly to the single FT-AN. In some instances, therapists will support parents to attend treatment days on their own, on condition that they, in conjunction with the MFT team, continue to expect the young person to attend and engage with the treatment.

The four-day intensive workshop
Structure
The four-day intensive workshop is the cornerstone of the MFT programme. The aim of the first four days is to provide intensive intervention to young people and their families to witness (observe), try out, reflect and learn new ways of working towards

recovery. It also creates an opportunity to reduce isolation, learn from others and have an additional therapy time and space to think about difficulties outside the eating disorder.

The workshop runs for four consecutive days in the week directly following the introductory afternoon, so as not to lose momentum from the engagement and energy created by the initial meeting. Each day begins at 10 a.m. and finishes at 4 p.m. with a break in the middle of the day after lunch. The room is set up in a circle with enough chairs for all participants and staff so that the day can begin and end with all together. Additional room is needed for separate activities with young people and parents (and siblings when they attend).

Each day consists of an introductory/opening activity, two longer activities and a shorter closing activity. The group will also eat morning snack, lunch and afternoon snack together. See some proposed times for how each day is usually structured:

As indicated in Table 5.1, the group is very activity based. The content of these activities is based around the principles of FT-AN and follows the phases of treatment, starting from engagement, moving to managing mealtimes, impact of the illness on family relationships, improving parental effectiveness around mealtimes, followed by moving the focus onto broader adolescent and family issues and, lastly, endings. For specific information on each activity and a clinician guide on when and how to choose them, and instructions how to run them, see Part II titled "MFT Activities" on p. 71.

Content

Group facilitators organise the content of MFT by first selecting themes for each MFT day. Themes should reflect shared treatment targets identified by the families attending MFT and be based in the principles of family therapy for anorexia nervosa. With a chosen theme in mind, specific activities are then selected for each day that are most likely to support discussion, experimentation and reflection around the chosen theme. This ensures that the group content is relevant to participants and that FT-AN and MFT-AN treatment goals are aligned and intensify and reinforce each other (see Table 5.2 and Table 5.3). The various activities that therapists can use during MFT are described in Part II of this book. The activities in Part II are organised according to themes. During each MFT day it is important that facilitators are open to feedback about the appropriateness of the chosen theme and flexibly adjust activities accordingly. Later on in treatment themes are typically more collaboratively generated with the group. For example, the whole group might discuss and decide which themes are important to address on the day or at the next follow-up day together. Please see Table 5.2 for example themes for the four-day intensive workshop.

The use of experiential, activity-based tasks is done with a particular purpose as it creates a context shift from the family therapy that families are already engaged in. It allows participants to learn, experience and reflect in novel ways to create new meaning and change. The main purpose of MFT is much broader than a support or psychoeducational group, and it should not be conducted solely as a series of group discussions in a wide circle. Activities may include the whole MFT group together, separate, parallel groups for parents and young people (sometimes also separate groups for fathers, mothers and siblings) or each family individually. See p. 58 for a detailed discussion and guide to clinician use of process issues that may arise from this unique treatment format and setting.

Theory, structure and techniques

Table 5.2 **Example themes for the four-day intensive**

Day	Theme
1	Engagement and understanding the illness and its impact
2	Managing mealtimes/supporting parents and YP to manage mealtimes more effectively
3	The impact of anorexia nervosa on family relationships and how to improve them
4	Looking ahead/the future

Quick Reference Box 5.2 **The four-day intensive workshop**

Quick Reference Box: The four-day intensive workshop	
Aims	• Provide intensive intervention to young people and families to witness, try out, reflect and learn new ways of managing the illness as individuals and as a family/team • Allow participants to learn from others who may be experiencing similar difficulties • Reduce isolation by creating connection with others and building a community of support • Provide space to offer practical support at mealtimes and during times of distress
Timing and structure	• 4 consecutive days • 10 a.m. – 4 p.m. • 3 meals per day • break after lunch
Content	• FT-AN principles • Psychoeducation about the illness • Impact of illness on family life • Managing mealtimes • Family strengths • Supporting family members (parents and siblings) • Instilling hope and future timeframe – needs to correspond to goals
Process	• Very structured and more planned • Staff directed • MFT group starts together at the beginning and end of each day • The whole MFT team also meets prior to the beginning and after the end of group each day during the group sessions • Mixture of modes of delivery, e.g. activity-based, experiential tasks, large group and separate groups for YP and parents, tasks for single families, with feedback to wider group, tasks for "foster families"

The four-day intensive workshop is initially highly structured and directed by the MFT team, with approximate timings of activities, meals and breaks clearly communicated ahead of time. This is done very intentionally, as it initially creates consistency, predictability, and boundaries, promoting emotional safety and the willingness from participants to try new things. This is also supported by the confident and warm manner of the MFT facilitators. The need for a pre-planned structure reduces as the group progresses over the four consecutive days; however, the MFT team will remain somewhat in charge throughout the initial four days with far more opportunity for flexibility in choice of activities during the follow-up days.

MFT-AN structure and content

Quick Reference Box 5.3 **Change in therapeutic alliance over the course of MFT**

Quick Reference Box: Change in therapeutic alliance over the course of MFT	
Early in treatment	**Later in treatment**
Staff act more as experts	More team discussion/less guided group discussions
Group more dependent on facilitators	Position of safe uncertainty, autonomy and decreased dependency on facilitators to guide the process
Facilitators approach more directive and didactic	More reflective stance
More visibly united MFT team	Public MFT team discussions and resolution of potential differences in views

Follow-up days

The aim of the follow-up days, the third component of MFT-AN, is to broaden the treatment focus beyond the eating disorder and to start to address any other adolescent or family issues that may be maintaining the illness. Activities and conversations are directed towards supporting greater adolescent autonomy, independence and social connectedness. In short, they are supported to integrate back to their "normal life" and therapeutic work focuses on and encourages greater emotional and social maturity.

For the parents in the group, the follow-up days serve to encourage everyone to regain their own space both as individuals and as couples. This might include having some personal time separate from the young people and support them in getting their own "life back". They are helped to "let go" of their, now unwarranted, extreme anxieties around their child's ability to be independent, and autonomous.

Group cohesion and mutual support will usually continue to deepen over the follow-up days, which allows even greater expression of feelings and the experience of feeling safe within the group, even when disclosing individual vulnerabilities. It is not uncommon for families to have started meeting outside of the organised MFT-AN days or to have contact, usually through e-mail or social media. While this is not necessarily encouraged with young people, it should not be shied away from and the pros and cons can be discussed as a group, especially for young people connecting through social media, as this can trigger unhelpful competitiveness regarding illness behaviours.

Over the course of the follow-up days, young people usually achieve greater flexibility with their meals and the MFT exercises also become more flexible. Nonetheless, their critical component remains; namely, to attempt new behaviours and learn to take new risks. Flexibility is fostered and new experiments tackle the intolerance of uncertainty and rigidity that are very often present in young people with anorexia nervosa and are reflected in their personal and family life. Therapists should start discussions in the group on the separation of illness behaviours from adolescent behaviours and question if the externalisation of the illness applies to all adolescents' behaviours.

There are usually four to six follow-up days offered over the period of six to eight months. The number of follow-up days can be decided by the team together with the group and should be based upon the cohesion of the group, speed of recovery and attendance patterns. Follow-up days initially occur close together (one to three weeks apart) and slowly become more and more spread out (up to eight weeks) by the end of treatment. This is done to promote the participant's own strengths, problem-solving skills and capacities, and to reduce dependence upon treatment and on the treating team. The

Theory, structure and techniques

Quick Reference Box 5.4 **Follow-up days**

Quick Reference Box: Follow-up days	
Aims	Support ongoing change and experimentation
	Begin to address issues beyond the eating disorder
	Support families to take ownership of the process and recovery
	Promote family independence and ending treatment
Timing and structure	One day each – stand alone
	10 a.m. – 4 p.m.
	Three meals
	Break after lunch
	Initially closer together (1–3 weeks) and then move further apart (4–6 weeks)
Content	Each day has a theme that guides content
	More flexible with content and can shift depending on group needs
	More focus on healthy adolescent development and family lifecycles rather than illness focus
	Relapse prevention and supporting positive help seeking
Process	Less structured – promote and model flexibility
	MFT group still begins and ends each day together to provide containment
	More directed by participants, with less staff direction
	More ownership of the MFT content and process by participants to a degree
	Frequency of follow ups spaced out as time goes on
	Promote self-reflection and problem solving, rather than staff providing answers

frequency of follow-up days is designed to replicate the family's progress in treatment and the move to independence.

Follow-up days are similar in structure to the days in the four-day intensive; however, as mentioned above, staff can be less didactic or directive, moving to a stance of being more reflective and supportive of group members using their own or each other's resources to solve any issues that arise. By the final follow-up day, the group process should be essentially handed over to the group to manage itself, without any input from the MFT team. See p. 29 for Quick Reference Box 5.3 for the change of therapeutic alliance over the course of MFT.

Just as with the four-day intensive workshop, follow-up days should have a theme decided upon by the team, with the potential to invite group members to provide ideas about what would be helpful or needed to inform the content of the future follow-up days. See Quick Reference Box 5.4 for an overview of the follow-up days. Themes should progressively move away from illness-related themes to broader adolescent and family lifecycle challenges. Themes remain a guide for MFT facilitators ensuring that all relevant areas for recovery from anorexia nervosa are covered over the course of MFT. For an example of the timing and themes for follow-up days see Table 5.3.

Table 5.3 **Example timing and themes for follow-up days**

Day	Timing	Theme
Follow up 1	1–2 weeks after four-day intensive workshop	Motivation, exploring and exiting rigid behaviour patterns, increasing mutual understanding
Follow up 2	2–3 weeks thereafter	Building relationships, social networks, and reflecting on body image
Follow up 3	3–4 weeks thereafter	Facing uncertainty, exploring independence, autonomy and use of social media
Follow up 4	4–5 weeks thereafter	Exploring journey through the illness and linking with the family lifecycle (past, present and future)
Follow up 5	5–6 weeks thereafter	Ending and life post anorexia nervosa
Follow up 6	7–8 weeks thereafter	Group will need six follow-up days only if some of the previous themes above had to be spread out over two follow-up days due to the speed of the change

Note

1 The Fifth Amendment in the US constitution allows individuals to refuse to answer questions that they think might "incriminate" them.

Chapter 6: The MFT treating team

The MFT treating team can be as little as two people but may include a number of professionals with varying levels of experience, skill and knowledge. As a minimum, the team consists of two lead facilitators, although it can be helpful to also have additional co-facilitators or helpers to ensure any unexpected things that arise may be dealt with, without needing to stop or take a break. Co-facilitators can be less experienced members of staff that have recently joined the team or trainees. Each team member has specific roles, which come together to ensure the process is navigated most effectively.

As a general rule, it is best not to have more staff members than there are families in the group. This is important in order for families not to feel like they are being "observed". With fewer facilitators each individual staff member will need to contribute more to the group, and by the same token will join the group process more. With too many staff members in the MFT treating team, each individual's contribution reduces, meaning that families may feel intensely observed, which may reduce a feeling of safety in the group.

MFT treating team members and roles
Lead facilitators
Key tasks

- Lead all clinical aspects of the group
- Contain the group and create an environment of safety that promotes discussion and change
- Facilitate activities

MFT is always run with two lead facilitators. It is their job to lead the group process and make decisions about all aspects of running the group in consultation with their team. They are responsible for providing containment to the group and monitoring the group process. In order to do this, lead facilitators would usually begin and end each day of MFT and might like to sit together or opposite each other during the early parts of treatment to promote the idea that they are working together to lead the group. They will also introduce, facilitate and debrief the majority of activities throughout the treatment. It is their task to manage the process and level of affect in the room, which they do by moving between direct teaching, feedback and reflection throughout the day. It is important that therapists support one another to reflect on their roles and decision-making, especially in relation to how they interact with the group or manage a potential conflict or discomfort. This requires a high level of collaborative working and trust between the therapists but also a high level of individual self-reflection and sensitivity to the group processes as they

The MFT treating team

unfold and develop. It is helpful to remember that working with tensions, discomfort, themes and dynamics is an integral part of any group work.

Co-facilitators and helpers

Key tasks

- Support lead facilitators
- Monitor group process and feedback to lead facilitators
- Lead tasks as required

The co-facilitators are responsible for supporting the lead facilitators and families throughout MFT. They are usually less active in the group and spend more time observing and feeding back to the lead facilitators. Their role is to keep an eye on any changes in content or process in the group and to provide support as appropriate. This might mean helping out with practical tasks, checking in on a particular person or family during a task or feeding back something to the facilitators during a break or a quiet moment. Co-facilitators may also introduce, run and debrief specific tasks throughout the group as decided upon with the lead facilitators. This may include leading the whole group through an activity or leading a subgroup when an activity is run with smaller groups.

One of the most important roles of the co-facilitators is that they can manage any unexpected things that may arise, while lead facilitators continue with the whole group. This is a key role of the co-facilitators as this function allows for the group process to be maintained should anything arise.

Co-facilitators may be team members, or family therapy, psychology and psychiatry trainees on placement with the team. It may be quite common to have observers or students join a group to learn about the treatment. This is appropriate and encouraged; however, lead facilitators need to think carefully about how much input different team members have and how they are referred to. Using the term "observers" again might make families feel as though they are "on show". The term "helper" or co-facilitator may help to reduce this feeling and promote safety within the group.

It will be important that all team members, regardless of experience or skill level, have some involvement with the group to ensure it feels as though the group is joining together. If a team member stays completely silent throughout the treatment and does not interact with any of the group members, the group process may become disjointed and difficult to manage.

Before the group begins, the lead facilitators should meet with any group "helpers" (and observers if attending). The helpers should be advised that attendance in the process is for the first four days and preferably for all of the follow-up days (in order to maintain consistency and a sense of safety for the families attending). They should also be told that while they may sometimes be asked to support families and separated groups with some of the tasks, decisions and specific requests for advice should be directed to the lead therapists. This is especially important for helpers who have not been previously involved in the MFT process and for whom group processes, rules and boundaries might be unclear.

Group coordinator/administrator

Key tasks

- Coordinate and organise practical elements of the group
- Be in charge of patient journey

Theory, structure and techniques

There is a third role within the group, the group coordinator. Their role is to be the contact person for the group and to manage all administrative and practical aspects of the group. This includes contacting the families and providing information when setting up the group or between follow-up days. It is also expected that FT-AN therapists who refer families for MFT will allow time in single-family sessions to answer any queries that families might have about MFT.

The group coordinator/administrator's role is to manage the practical aspects of the young person and family's "journey" over the course of the treatment. This role may be taken on by one of the lead or co-facilitators, or may be done by your clinical administrative team. If you decide to have this role taken on by an administrator, they will need clear guidance and direction on how to manage the treatment set-up, how to talk about the group and the expectations of families.

MFT team functioning

Facilitating MFT requires the MFT team to be aware of multiple processes occurring simultaneously. The team running MFT are responsible for creating a space for the families in which they can feel supported to learn and try out new behaviours, ways of thinking and expressing different emotions. In order to do this the facilitators must manage the group process, which is constantly oscillating between the validation of the participant's multiple experiences in the room and the difficulties they face, as well as expecting change and movement. This is an important and often difficult thing to do when facilitating the group, as there are multiple processes and systems at play throughout.

The team must also be mindful of their own unique knowledge, skills and personalities and what these characteristics bring to the group. In many ways the treating team is like an extra "family" in the group dynamic and should not be underestimated or dismissed when thinking about the group and its planning. At times staff members will engage in different activities or join the process in other ways. The staff experience of the group may parallel that of the families in that they will need to constantly move flexibly in and out of different roles, e.g. leading activities, being didactic, listening, reflecting, witnessing, learning, leaning into affect, sharing personal experiences as appropriate. As such, being mindful of inter and intra team processes is key.

The most effective way to manage this complex process is to ensure that the team is well prepared for the group and that they are discussing the group throughout the day and over the course of treatment.

Pre-MFT preparation

In order to ensure the team is well prepared for running the MFT group, it is important that each individual member has a good understanding of the participants, and that the team have met to plan the group. Individually each team member should be up to date with each young person and their family, including current concerns, history of symptoms, change points in their history and any familial or context issues. This will include a thorough risk assessment and understanding of any potential risks. This may include reading all of the assessment reports and getting a good handover from their FT-AN clinician.

Note-taking should be shared between the group facilitators and helpers. The requirements for the recording of clinical notes will vary dependent on service setting. Good written notes are invaluable as a way of following the development of the group but also for planning future follow-ups. Good clinical notes from MFT are also essential for keeping the treating therapist up to date with developments and progress in the MFT. As a minimum it is recommended to record who attended, which activities were completed, which meals were had and what was eaten, and the families' response to the day.

A large lockable cupboard and portfolios for each MFT group can be really useful in order to store the group's drawings or handwritten work safely over the months of the group. It is important for families to know that the handwritten work they created during the group will be kept confidential and looked after carefully over the course of the group. At the end of the group, families can be offered the choice of taking their handwritten work home or allowing the clinic to dispose of it securely. Bringing out some of their handwritten work, for example "timelines" from the first four days, at the end of MFT follow-ups can be a helpful part of the process of reflection on progress and therefore this work needs to be readily available for follow-up tasks. It can also be important to allow families to take work home straight away as reminders of work done in the group and therapeutic goals that were set up in between follow ups.

A dedicated resource cupboard or other form of storage is helpful. Plans for specific tasks can be made on the day in response to new information, so a readily available store of often-used materials allows for this flexibility. Here is a list of pre-group tasks.

Pre-group tasks
1. Read everyone's assessment information.
2. Get an up-to-date handover of response to treatment with individual clinicians.
3. Get an up-to-date risk assessment.
4. Meet as a team to discuss each individual young person and family, their treatment needs, risk and individual team member roles.
5. Check that the materials cupboard is well stocked with all the materials required for the four days and follow ups.

When to meet as a team during MFT
Throughout the MFT treatment one of the most important things outside of facilitating the group is for the MFT team to regularly talk to each other. Staff must schedule a time to meet away from the group at least three times per day, as well as any additional ad hoc conversations that are required. Meeting should occur:

- Before the group starts each day (30 min.)
- During the break after lunch (30 min.)
- At the end of the day (30–45 min.)
- Ad hoc (as needed)

Content of MFT team meetings
Each of the MFT team meetings away from the families has a distinct content and role. At the start of the day, lead therapists and helpers will spend more time planning the structure and content of the coming day. Meeting and discussion at various points throughout the day and at the end of each day will be more for debriefing and reflection. Lead therapists should seek helpers' views and reflections as they may have a unique position in sometimes observing the process and having helpful ideas in this respect.

Team discussion and reflections should involve practical, clinical, group dynamic and team dynamic aspects of the day. Each of these aspects should be touched upon as quickly or as in depth as is required at any one time. The principal guideline is to structure these meetings in a way to ensure that as little is missed as possible. Practical elements

Theory, structure and techniques

of the discussion should be aimed at planning anything upcoming for the day or until the next break, make sure staff know what each person is doing and ensure that the required resources are available. The conversation will then steer towards any clinical updates that may be required. This will include quickly mentioning each young person and their family to check in with the team about response and progress to date. This will then help to inform ongoing hypotheses and needs for the group.

Once the practical and clinical items have been discussed it is also important to discuss process – both group and team dynamics. Group process discussions should touch upon where the level of engagement is for the group, other dynamics, and whether the level of affect in the room is too high, low or at the right level to be conducive to change. Team process discussions are also important and will include how the team is working together, where everyone's energy, understanding and confidence is at. Lastly, reflections can be made about how the team is managing the group at large. These conversations do not need to be formal, or follow a strict structure, however, it is important that they occur regularly and each of the areas are at least touched upon. Quick Reference Box 6.1 provides a structure for team meetings at the beginning, middle and end of each day.

As in any other therapeutic activity, clinicians will have their own self-reflections of the impact of the group and team dynamics on themselves and where appropriate these may sometimes be usefully shared with other team members. Sharing such self-reflections will often be fairly brief and may not have a central role in the team discussions while the group is running. There will be occasions when there is a need for addressing such issues in greater depth, i.e. when the team dynamic is blocking or negatively impacting the whole group. Where possible, this should be done at the end of the day meeting or in a separate supervisory context as described below.

Quick Reference Box 6.1 **Team discussions – key topics**

Quick Reference Box: Team discussions – key topics	
Practical tasks	- Ensure theme(s) for the day have been identified - Plan activities for the day - Allocate staff to activities and families as needed - Ensure resources and materials are available
Clinical tasks	- Discuss each YP and family and their response to treatment - Update hypotheses and formulations - Identify learning points for tasks/day - Allocate families to specific task as required (e.g. foster families)
Group processes	- Engagement - Check in about group dynamics, process, affect - Reflect on group cohesions - Take note of any conflict(s) or tension
Team processes	- Understanding of the tasks - Team confidence - Team energy - Document any observations/processes/ideas - Differences in opinions - Team dynamic

Ad hoc and unplanned meetings during MFT

Given the complex nature of MFT and the multiple processes occurring at once, it will be inevitable that team members need to catch up with each other throughout the day for quick, ad hoc discussions around how the group is progressing. Things that might spark a conversation include a team member noticing a change in group process, observing and identifying an important moment that can be built upon, one particular individual or family beginning to struggle, or a risk issue presenting itself. If this occurs, it will be important to alert the lead facilitator(s) who can then have a quick discussion and make a decision about how to potentially modify an activity. This can be done in private by slightly removing oneself from an activity, or in private with group facilitators discussing it while families are involved in group activity on their own. Another way to manage this might be to gently pause the activity and have a discussion that is witnessed by the group. Once facilitators become more familiar and comfortable with the process, discussing openly what they have observed in front of the group can become quite a powerful tool as it will model problem-solving to the group as well as identifying when and how to shift the focus effectively in response to the families' feedback and responses.

Clinical supervision and consultation

In addition, to the team meeting process described (see p. 36), which is the minimum level of clinical reflection required, there is a role for more formal clinical supervision both prior and during the MFT group under certain circumstances. When a team is in the early phases of implementing MFT then the input of a more experienced clinician will be invaluable from a clinical, planning and problem-solving point of view.

Similarly, if the lead facilitators are new to the role then additional input to help support their role will be of benefit. It will also be important if the group seems to be experiencing a dynamic that is hard to understand or manage, and thus some input outside of the current MFT facilitator team will add a broader perspective. Supervision as described here may need to occur at the beginning and end of the day during a group or alternatively it may be a one-off consultation during a group.

Facilitating MFT is a complex endeavour and clinicians will, from time to time, experience anxiety about their management of a group. This is often most noticeable when debriefing. We may feel a sense of uncertainty or lack of clarity about what we are trying to draw out of the group, or it may be something about our own life that is triggered. In some ways we experience a version of what the families feel in the group, and the ability to contain these feelings in the moment and remain "in" the group and on track is important.

While there is not space to address the myriad of ways we can be affected as facilitators, it is a reminder that clinicians should be taking MFT to their individual supervision if there is a recurring issue they are identifying. However, MFT group reflection and supervision that occurs during the programme should be seen as the primary place for reflection on the families and the associated group dynamics and processes.

Chapter 7: Managing process and group facilitation

With multiple families in the room, multiple processes occurring simultaneously, and the use of activity or experiential tasks as part of the treatment, MFT may feel very new and overwhelming for clinicians. While it is true that multiple things are happening at once, over time and with experience, clinicians will begin to be able to navigate this process in a useful way and feel more confident and trusting of the process.

Facilitating MFT will feel quite different to running individual or single-family therapy. Unlike in other settings, MFT requires the facilitators to enable and promote discussion *between* group members, not just between the facilitators and individuals/single families. At the very beginning of treatment and while the group is forming, the facilitators will need to direct conversation far more than later on in the process; however, they should always keep in mind that discussion between the group members should be promoted from very early on. Later on, the main role of facilitators will be to introduce new ideas or concepts, while the group members will have been enabled to navigate the discussion successfully together, allowing the facilitators to step back from the process. The role of the therapist is to move from being quite involved at the beginning of treatment to the position of hovering more on the periphery towards the end. No matter how distant, however, staff should always be at the disposal of the group to briefly dip in as needed, to steer the content or process back on track – but only as needed.

An MFT clinician has several clinical tools in their toolbox (Figure 7.1). There are elements of the content, process and structure (e.g. setting/physical environment etc.) at their disposal, as well as the timing and pace in which it is delivered. The next section, "Choosing activities", is an outline on how to use these tools effectively to navigate treatment context, how to choose which activities to include each day, how to facilitate them in a way that promotes change and what to do if it does not go quite according to plan.

Choosing activities

Deciding which activities to include each day in MFT is an important team process that requires specific attention regardless of whether it is the first day or the final follow-up day. Just as the initial days in treatment are more structured, the content is also more pre-determined and planned. When it comes to deciding what to include in the follow-up days, however, there is a lot more freedom and flexibility – which can bring with it a lot of clinician anxiety and uncertainty. See Quick Reference Box 7.1 on p. 39 for assistance in deciding how to choose activities. Using the five key questions from the quick reference box may guide the MFT team decision on what the most helpful theme(s) are to explore for the day.

Managing process and group facilitation

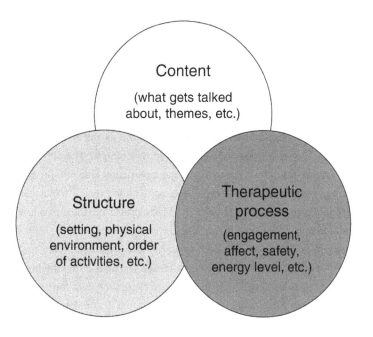

7.1
MFT clinician toolkit

Quick Reference Box 7.1 **A guide to choosing MFT activities**

	Quick Reference Box A guide to choosing MFT activities
1.	Reflect as a team using five key questions beforehand a) What are the needs of each young person and their family? b) What are the needs of the group? c) Is it the early, middle or end phase of MFT-AN? d) What stage of recovery are group participants in? e) How cohesive and engaged is the group?
2.	Choose theme(s) for the day
3.	Choose activities for the day that: – generate content related to identified themes – are varied enough from each other – in either content, mode of delivery or structure
4.	Reflect as a team on what did and did not work so well to ensure MFT team and treatment development

Once the theme(s) are established, an appropriate set of activities can be chosen that will best facilitate discussion and reflection around this. It will be important to have activities that do not feel too similar in their content or structure so as to reduce potential for treatment to feel repetitious, familiar, predictable or boring. Remember, families are together for a long time each day, potentially for several days in a row, so there is a need to be dynamic in order to keep up the energy in the room to generate new ideas. The structure of each day and the predictable timings of activities and meals creates safety, so the activities themselves are a place to experiment with change. This is achieved by choosing activities with varying content, formats and modes of delivery (e.g. talking, writing, small groups, separate groups, moving around etc.).

There is no "right" or "wrong" way to choose the activities for a day; however, some activities will be better suited to earlier or later in MFT-AN. The key is to experiment with what works well together and to learn from trying out new things. It is a flexible model and should not be too rigid.

Theory, structure and techniques

Facilitating activities

While each MFT activity requires different elements to be prepared (which is detailed in Part II of this manual), there are some elements and techniques common to the way all activities are facilitated. Most notably, every MFT activity once chosen has subsequent steps to be followed starting with the preparation, setting up, executing/carrying it out, observing the group's response and finishing with reflection and debriefing (Figure 7.2).

The first tasks in facilitating an activity are to ensure the aim of the activity is clearly identified – essentially, what is hoped to be achieved by doing it? The aim can vary significantly and may range from the need to introduce a particular idea into the group, such as the importance of parents presenting a consistent parenting team, to increasing hope, building understanding, or motivating action. This is important to decide as a team so that the set-up, execution and debrief can be guided to reach this target.

With the aim in mind, the team will then need to have materials ready and room(s) available to allow the activity to take place. When facilitating an activity, the first task is to set it up with the group. This is usually done in a large circle with everyone present, even if the activity involves breaking away into separate groups. The reason for introducing the activity to the whole group is twofold; firstly, it means everyone receives the same instructions, and secondly, it creates structure and containment by marking the beginning of the task and the end of the previous task.

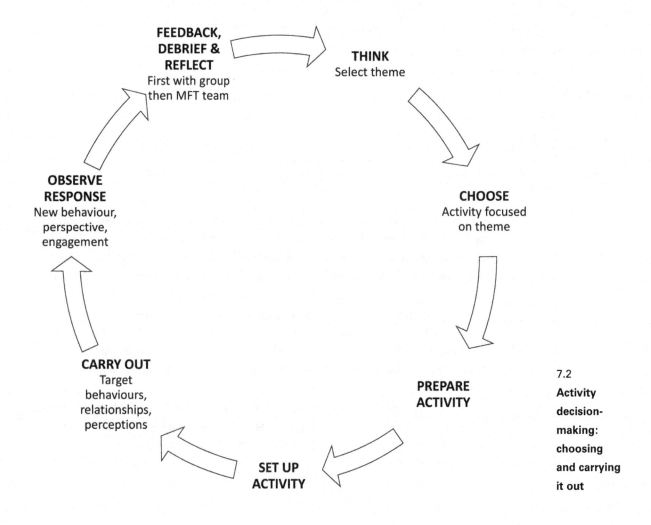

7.2 Activity decision-making: choosing and carrying it out

Managing process and group facilitation

Initially, activities are usually introduced by the lead facilitators; however, this may extend to co-facilitators as the group progresses. Early on in MFT it will be important to give clear, confident instructions to ensure that the participants feel contained by the team; however, more flexibility and less guidance will be important as treatment progresses.

Once the activity is set up, participants then engage in the activity itself, whether that is working individually, working in a small group or engaging in a particular type of discussion. During this part of any activity, it is usually the job of the facilitators to support individuals or groups to complete and/or troubleshoot the content of the task as needed. This may require quite active involvement during each step of the task in hand. If the activity requires group work, similar to the way that meals are facilitated, support is offered by visiting different subgroups of people to briefly check-in and problem-solve as needed and then to step back to allow the participants to continue with the task. When not directly interacting with a group or individual, facilitators will hover around the room, monitoring group process and progress. Asen and Scholz (2010) describe this process as being like a bird that is circling the group, swooping in and out as needed. It is also important to give time warnings so that people know how quickly or slowly they need to work.

Once everyone has completed the activity or the allocated time is nearing an end, it is then important to move into finishing the activity with a debrief. The purpose of the debrief is to share new learning, experiences and ideas from individuals or small subgroups with the group as a whole. Typically, this involves asking individuals or smaller groups to reflect on the task with the wider group. This is a very important part of each activity as it allows for different perspectives and experiences to be heard and learned from. The job of the facilitators will be to guide reflections and new learning based on the aims of the task, the theme of the day and the need of the group at that moment.

Getting feedback about activities in MFT is usually the most important task for facilitators. In many ways, the task itself is less important than the learning, reflection and meaning that comes out of the activity – all likely to resonate with participants. Be strategic when debriefing. Not everybody needs to provide feedback. Even if only a few participants speak, the rest of the group is listening.

Things to consider might be (see Figure 7.3):

- Who to start and end with?
- What message do you want the activity to end on?
- Where do similarities and differences lie in the group?
- What will promote the most cross-family conversation? Is this helpful now?
- Does everyone need to give feedback, or are a few powerful words more meaningful?
- Would brief injections of psychoeducation or reflections from staff enhance the debrief?
- Does everything need to be resolved, or will the feedback be more meaningful if left open?
- Is it more strategic to leave the affect slightly higher in the group, rather than reducing it right now?
- If I leave things open now, do I have time later in the day to resolve this?
- What messages does the group need to hear?
- Which messages might be more helpful not to discuss at this point?

Theory, structure and techniques

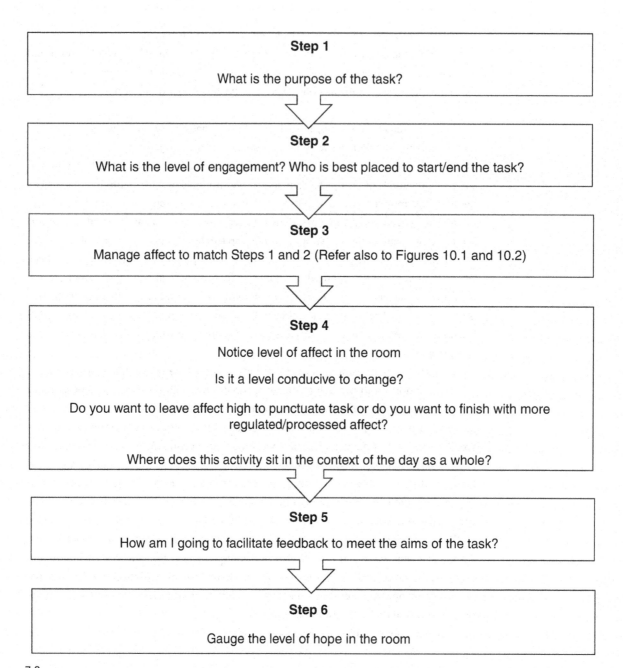

7.3
Clinician map to facilitating activities

Clinician map to facilitating activities

By holding these steps in mind, facilitators will turn the activities from an information sharing or support group, into rich therapeutic group work. Feedback and reflections with the group and debrief with the MFT team will also inform the team if the next planned activity is still well-suited for the current needs of the group. Debrief and reflection with the MFT team might indicate that some other activity needs to be considered from the diverse repertoire of activities described in Part II. However, facilitators might also decide to devise a new activity that has not been described in this manual, but that still targets themes outlined in this manual relevant to the phase and current needs of the group.

Managing process and group facilitation

How to develop a new activity

Creating new activities is a good way of ensuring that the team continues to be creative in their therapeutic approach and can deepen therapists' understanding of the MFT process. This is particularly useful for teams new to MFT but also for teams who feel that their work is becoming too routine or lacking in energy.

1. **Identify need**: What is the specific need that you wish to address? This may include needs addressed by existing activities, which you feel could be addressed better (or differently) for instance by having a stronger non-verbal component etc.
2. **Identify content**: Plan out content that needs covering and create specific aims for the activity. This will help shape how to structure thinking and decision-making around the rest of the planning.
3. **Participant mix**: Identify the participant mix (parents, YP, whole group, small mixed groups etc.). Changing participant mix or group size may provide alternative options for running an activity. Link this clearly with the aims of the activity. Consider who you are most trying to reach with this activity.
4. **Get creative**: Bring in process, structure, craft, environment, team elements to ensure the participants will *experience* the activity, not just *talk about* the content. Consider games, physical movement, use of silence etc. Think carefully about pace and intensity, particularly for non-verbal activities. This will help ensure the affect is pitched at a level to support reflection and change. Affect will hopefully change within the activity. It can be a mixture of fun, serious, silly, reflective etc.
5. **Consider feedback format**: As described on pp. 41–42, feedback is perhaps the most important part of any MFT activity. Ensure the feedback format helps to bring out the aims of the activity as fully as possible without constraining the process. Anticipate any difficulties, consider how to manage strong affect if needed and modify the plan as needed. Remember that the process of feedback is at least as important as its content. Feedback, at an early phase of a group will often work best if given to the whole group, whereas at later phases it may be simply between two or three families.
6. **Consider materials needed**.
7. **Write it down**: This includes writing out a structure for the activity as well as exact instructions on how to introduce the task to the group. This is especially helpful.
8. **Experiment**: Give it a go! This step involves finding a balance between sticking to your plan to see how it works, but also being open and flexible in response to anything unexpected that might arise when facilitating the activity. These could be content or process issues. Ask families to give feedback on their experience of the activity and whether it addressed the need that you had considered important.
9. **Review as a team**: Reflect together about content, process and affect. Did the activity meet the aims you set out to achieve? How did the group respond? Was the affect pitched at an appropriate level for change to occur etc.? This is a crucial step as it is the only way to ensure the activity continues to be refined and that knowledge from one group experience is extended to the wider team and MFT community.
10. **Document**: Ensure any learning or reflections are documented and any modifications to the original plan are incorporated.

Theory, structure and techniques

Position, proximity and focus

Using the physical space and environment is a powerful way to complement the content and to manage group processes during MFT. The team will need to be mindful of things such as:

- Where each member of the team sits or stands
- Whether they remain sitting or standing
- With whom they are talking (or not talking)
- Tone of voice
- The way in which they are directing conversation

Being purposeful in how these elements are used will help to validate and reinforce particular experiences or behaviours that enhance the group and/or extinguishing ones that do not. Using these factors in the group will help change the level of energy in the room.

When working with such a large group it is important to be mindful of where staff and families are placed, who to address and how. Placement in the room can impact on engagement, how intimate a conversation may feel and/or how different members of the group are perceived. Generally, when the whole group is together, all members of a family will tend to sit together unless specified. This may change as time goes on and the group becomes more familiar with one another. Staff, however, will usually spread themselves between the families to enhance the feeling of integration, rather than reinforcing the staff as a separate group – an "other". The lead facilitators may choose to sit together to start and end each day to promote the idea that they are working together, united and an effective team.

The lead facilitators might also decide to sit opposite one another if one of them is predominantly leading an activity. Sitting opposite one another allows the facilitator who leads the activity to get immediate non-verbal feedback (facial expressions, eye contact) from the other co-facilitator, which might communicate how the activity is going. Non-verbal communication between co-facilitators serves as an instant "checking in" of where the group process is going and the impact that the intervention and the other co-facilitator is having on the group. Sitting opposite also gives space to the other co-facilitator to step in, to either initiate a co-facilitators' face-to-face discussion and model how potential differences in perceptions are resolved within the co-facilitating pair, or to offer another view on the group process to the group.

When facilitating an activity, sitting close to someone can help to manage a process in many ways. For example, if a young person is struggling to speak in the wider group, a facilitator may strategically sit next to them to try and make any question directed towards them feel more private and manageable as a result of the proximity. Similarly, leaning in physically towards someone and holding eye contact if they are upset or struggling to speak might have a similar effect. Another reason for a facilitator to choose an individual or family to specifically sit next to might be that they will need to help out with the next activity, and it will make it easier to begin and ensure participation from the individual.

Similarly, staff may equally decide *not* to sit close to particular people, families or groups at various times. This could be for a whole number of reasons. One example might be that a particular person or family may have been the focus of a previous activity or discussion and may benefit from participating less for some time to reduce intensity.

Other reasons may include that there has been a lot of interaction between two particular people or groups and spreading people out may help to reduce the potential for alliances, coalitions or perceived favouritism. Staff may choose to spend more time with or sit closer to members of the group with whom they feel less engaged to try and enhance a connection.

In addition to proximity and position in the room, the way attention is focused can be used to similar effect by facilitators. The use of eye contact, tone of voice and, where particular questions are directed will help to shape and manage the group dynamics. Staff members may choose to start or end an activity with particular people. Some reasons to do this include how the previous task was managed, how present different people have been in the group, how much someone has been struggling, etc. Remember, most people will be listening, even if they appear not to be. A conversation may be had with one person with the specific purpose of someone nearby being able to hear it without having to be explicitly told. Likewise, facilitators can make use of private and public conversations to create feelings of cohesion or uniqueness.

The role and proximity of group facilitators and helpers is likely to differ depending on whether it is a facilitated group activity during the "official" group time compared to more informal interactions that occur during breaks (after meals, before the start, or at the end of the group). During informal interactions the MFT team displays a chatty, friendly and empathic attitude, engaging in social interactions that resemble much more spontaneous everyday social interaction, while still respecting and maintaining social norms and boundaries implied in a therapeutic relationship.

It would be impossible to list all of the ways and all of the reasons why position, proximity and focus can be harnessed by clinicians. Needless to say, once monitored, it can be a powerful way of enhancing the therapeutic work.

The use of self

Every clinician will come to MFT with their own unique personality, strengths, experience, ages, genders and blind spots. It is only natural and expected when running MFT that different team members will engage with the MFT content and team, individual group members and their families, or with the group as a whole in different ways (Figure 7.4). Individual clinicians will likely have different professional histories with different group members and may know some people quite well already. Similarly, certain staff will have worked together a lot, whereas some will be brand new to a team or used to working with a particular clinician. Each clinician will perform differently depending on with whom he/she is co-facilitating a group when each person's previous experience, personality and therapeutic style come into interplay.

An individual clinician's therapeutic style, personality and use of self are just as much a tool as all the other things listed in this manual and can be used to enhance the treatment. This might include assigning different team members' different roles, activities to run or families to keep more in mind. Play to each other's strengths while being mindful of the impact this may have on the group. Also bear in mind how these change as the group continues. As the treatment progresses some staff may end up forming closer therapeutic relationships with different group members. While not encouraged, if mindful of the impact on the group as a whole, individual engagement with certain people can be very useful for that person, their experience of treatment and recovery.

Theory, structure and techniques

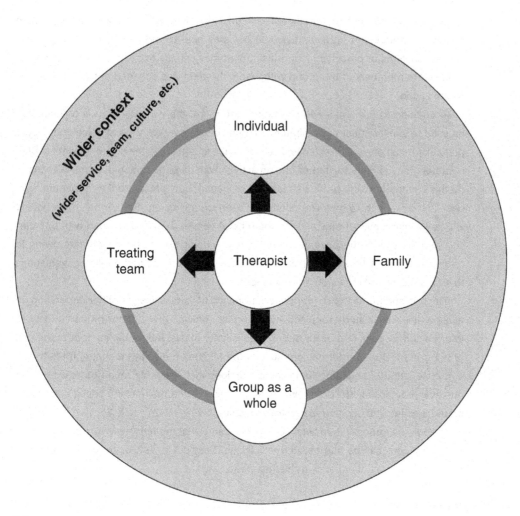

7.4
Therapist relationships in MFT

The use of humour and playfulness

Humour and playfulness have important and often helpful roles in MFT, whether introduced by the therapists or family members. Facilitators should be prepared to use humour, being mindful that it should be appropriate and timely. In the group, humour and playfulness can help in building and enhancing communication, fostering creativity, reducing resistance and tension, and increasing trust and cohesion. Humour and playfulness can also facilitate perceiving things from another perspective (mentalizing) and motivate families to participate in new tasks. Humour, of course, has its own pitfalls, particularly if used too frequently or in inappropriate situations, as it may block the deepening of affect or distract from a serious point. Many of the activities described in Part II encourage creativity and playfulness and often work best when participants engage with a degree of irreverence. This does not preclude encouraging reflections during feedback that can lead to important insights, new connections, learning and the new choice of activities initiated by the facilitators.

Chapter 8: Therapeutic techniques

There are a range of therapeutic techniques that are unique to the MFT context. These techniques can be used to manage different aspects of the group process, such as improving group cohesion, managing affect, offering containment, increasing level of energy, therapeutically getting people out of their comfort zone, helping participants to take different perspectives, to experiment and be playful and so on. Several are outlined in this chapter; however, there are many more. One thing about MFT is that it is a good format for experimentation. Try things out and document them so that they can be enhanced in the future.

Interviewing techniques

Many of the techniques used in MFT are extensions of single-family therapy interviewing techniques such as circular, reflexive, strategic or future-oriented questions, conversations that map the effects of the illness on the family, exploration of patterns of interactions, attending to beliefs, behaviours, emotions and feelings. These techniques are well described in the literature and will not be elaborated here (Eisler & Lask 2008; Eisler et al., 2016b). Engaging a group of families has a number of distinct features. In the early phase, the therapists' key goal is engaging all the families. At the same time, it is important from the beginning to support the development of a sense of connectedness between families through the sharing of their specific experiences.

Keeping connected with individuals, individual families and the group as a whole

Therapists who are used to working with families will be familiar with the need to maintain awareness and connection with the whole family, for instance not keeping their eyes completely fixed on the person they are talking to but also making at least brief eye contact with others. In the MFT group, therapists have to learn to scan the whole group allowing the focus of their attention to move around the group, both to have an awareness of what's going on and also to signal their connectedness with the group as a whole rather than just with individual group members. There will of course be moments when the therapists focus on a particular family or an individual, but this will always be followed by a broadening out of the conversation to include the larger group. This moving in and out may happen purely through the way conversations are focused or may be done more purposefully. For example, a therapist may intentionally stand or sit next to a family briefly to start a more focused conversation, and then move away encouraging the conversation to continue within the family or with those close by. It is important to note here the

Theory, structure and techniques

complementary role that the co-facilitators have in ensuring that the group as a whole is kept in mind.

Connecting families with families

When the whole MFT group is together there will typically be 20–30 people in the room and if the therapist is too central and most of the conversations are happening between therapist and individual families most of the group will be observing rather than actively participating. To avoid this, therapists have to actively invite interaction between families. This can happen in a number of ways.

Eliciting themes across families

While talking to family A the therapist may notice other people in the room responding non-verbally: "*I noticed that when Mrs A was commenting on the difficulty dad was having in talking to Jenny, several of the dads were nodding. Is this something that is often happening between fathers and daughters?*" This may generate a conversation across the group as a whole or the therapist may invite comments from fathers, mothers and young people separately to get their different perspectives.

Creating subgroups in the large group

Once families have become familiar with the way therapists elicit feedback following different exercises, families can be invited to debrief by talking to another family rather than talking in the large group. Similarly, in the previous example, the therapist could have asked fathers, mothers and the young people to discuss the question in small groups before feeding back to the larger group.

Connections and differences in the here and now and over time

Both the shared and the unique experiences that each person identifies when talking to others in the MFT group are important and the therapists work purposefully for these to be made visible and available as a resource for others. The connections that people make will not only be in the here and now but also over time. For instance, in an early session many of the young people may be sceptical that change is possible and be very dismissive about the group saying they were only there because their parents insisted. The therapist, aware that this was shared by most but not all, might comment: "*When Annie said that she was only here because she had her arm twisted behind her back, I had a sense that she wasn't speaking just for herself. Do people agree?*" (checking with first the young people who are likely to agree before turning to someone who had indicated that she wants to get better). "*Jenny, you said that you are here because you want to get better. I wonder when you look back can you think of a time when you would have said the same as Annie? How did you get from there to where you are now? What has made the difference?*" If any of the young people (or their parents) who were negative about the group earlier continue to be dismissive, the therapists should acknowledge that not everyone finds MFT helpful even though many do. If appropriate the therapist might ask one of them.

Balancing expertise with lived experience

There will be frequent occasions when the therapists will be invited to offer their expertise (about the causes of anorexia nervosa, likelihood of recovery, what is a healthy weight etc.). This puts therapists in a bind because on the one hand providing expertise provides containment and is often a helpful part of ongoing psychoeducation but on the other hand it puts the therapists centre stage and participants may perceive that they have all the answers. Feedback from families shows (Salaminiou et al., 2017) that they find therapists' expert knowledge reassuring but also value the openness of therapist to the limitations of their knowledge. This includes an acknowledgement that even the best research evidence does not apply in the same way to everyone individually.

In giving information it is, therefore, important to combine it with a discussion with the families as to how they think it may apply to them. Therapists can also use their expertise from having met large numbers of families and being aware of the variability of people's experiences. Checking individual experiences is especially important when related to the young person, particularly when there might be stereotypical expectations. For example, the technique of externalisation has been shown to be an effective intervention for adolescent anorexia nervosa (Ellison et al., 2012), but clinical experience shows that many adolescents dislike it especially if it is done in the form of giving anorexia nervosa a name or describing it as a voice. A conversation along the following lines can be helpful:

> *Several people have now talked about anorexia as if it had a voice or even as if it was somehow a separate person. Does that make sense to people? ... We know both from research and from talking to families that for many it is a helpful idea but a number of young people dislike it. What is it like for you?* (inviting each young person by name in turn to comment).

This will often generate a conversation about why it might be helpful (it makes it possible to talk about anorexia nervosa without feeling blamed, it allows people to have a sense that they can fight back and have some control over getting their life back etc.). This can also encourage true mentalization on the part of the parents rather than hyper mentalization (when we think we know what the other person feels or thinks but we are wrong). Therapists should use their expertise to explain that what young people are describing are anorexic cognitions, e.g. persistent, intrusive thoughts that are part of the illness and are different from "hearing voices". This can be reassuring for most of the young people in the group, and more consistent with their experience.

Specific techniques
Fishbowl/Reflecting team/Using a one-way mirror

Fishbowls, reflecting teams and using one-way mirrors are techniques commonly used in MFT as a way of having conversation with one part of the group while it is witnessed by other parts of the group. This is a useful way of highlighting a particular event or theme, or a means of putting "heat on" or taking "heat off" a certain group or topic. A fishbowl is when a smaller circle is created inside the wider circle who then listen in as the inner circle have a "private" conversation. A similar situation can be created using reflecting teams and one-way mirrors where one group observes another via various means.

Fishbowls and related techniques are commonly used in MFT and are a powerful way of helping a particular group have a voice and be witnessed in expressing that voice (e.g. young people with the illness, mothers, siblings etc.). A fishbowl is set up by inviting the identified group to "bring their chairs into the middle of the group to make a circle". While participants may initially find this uncomfortable, it does not take long for people to

Theory, structure and techniques

participate. The conversation would usually revolve around a particular topic or reflection from an activity. Once the conversation is finished, the smaller group then rejoins the wider circle and a reflection is invited from the "witnesses".

A reflecting team is often used when the MFT team or staff are the group in the middle of the circle having the discussion. This might be used as a way of giving feedback to the group in a way that feels less threatening and new. Staff are cautious to frame any feedback as tentative and hypotheses, rather than truth.

Lastly, one-way mirrors can be used to make the separation feel even slightly more pronounced. Instead of the whole group being in the same room during the task, the group having a discussion is in one room, while the "witnessing" group is behind the one-way screen. As with the fishbowl, if a conversation is witnessed either using a one-way mirror or as a reflecting team, it is important to get feedback from the witnessing group so that the group rejoins by the end of the activity.

Role play/Role reversal

Role plays and role reversals are a powerful way of exploring new content and themes in a very experiential way. Role plays and role reversals may be used in two very useful ways. Firstly, they may be used to help participants not just hear about what something is like from another's perspective but to *experience* this for themselves. Secondly, role plays or reversals may be used to create a situation whereby participants are provided the freedom and permission to test out new behaviours or talk about new things while "being" somebody else. Feedback from participants is that role plays and reversals not only help to cognitively understand something, but really "get it". This can be a powerful tool to foster empathy and validation for all group members and is a key part of what makes the group experience unique.

Mixed family groups and "foster families"

Foster families is a technique whereby small groups are created that include people from different families to resemble a new "foster family" for the purposes of a particular activity. For example, a foster family might include a young person with anorexia nervosa, a different group member's mother, and a different group member's father – i.e. three people from three different families. For other activities larger mixed family groups can be created using the same principle – i.e. each group having no more than one person from any family. Foster families use positive peer and group pressures to help participants start to practise sharing or trying out new things and validating their own and others' experiences. The unique environment created in a foster family means that people are often very polite, patient and caring of one another – potentially a new experience for all members if their own family is stressed, tired and in frequent conflict as a result of trying to manage the illness.

Choosing members of a foster family can be done strategically to achieve a certain dynamic or opportunity. While the example above is of a nuclear family, foster family members do not always have to resemble a participant's family of origin. Strategically, the MFT team might decide it will be more therapeutic not to. An example of this might be if there is significant sibling discord in one family, those siblings might enjoy the space and freedom of being in different families.

Small group huddle

This is a technique used to help generate concise feedback or reflections from particular groups or constellations of participants – whether it be pairs, a family huddle, a group of random participants or a group of people with particular roles. While it can be used at any time, it is most commonly used during ice-breakers or ending activities to get a reflection from the day or hearing a goal or action point for a particular group. Often the huddle is a family huddle, whereby facilitators might ask family members to come together for a few moments to discuss a specific question or generate a particular idea/response. Small group huddles can also be used if conversation in the wider group seems to be flat and people appear nervous or anxious about speaking. An example of when a family huddle might be used could be when ending the day and asking a family to come up with one thing they will try to do differently together that evening. The huddles are never very long, and the feedback should be brief and concise.

Spatial positioning

In this intervention participants are asked, without speaking, to position themselves in the physical space of the group room, according to how much they agree or disagree with a statement that is read out loud by the facilitators. The space in the group room is set up so that one side of the room represents a "strongly agree" viewpoint and the opposite side a "strongly disagree". Once everyone has had a chance to think about the statement and place themselves according to their own opinion, the facilitators can then move around the room enquiring of the thinking behind the response. If appropriate facilitators may ask the participants where they think the facilitators would place themselves in the room to determine whether participants think they are thinking in similar ways to professionals.

Spatial position is an important technique used in MFT as it is a quick way to simultaneously find out what everyone in the group is thinking on the particular topic. All participants, not just facilitators, will be able to visually understand what everyone else in the room is thinking. This is very useful as it helps to quickly determine a snapshot for where the group is up to and the level of understanding. It is also a powerful way of opening a discussion about why different people were thinking, behaving or feeling in a certain way. Lastly, it opens up a discussion between participants to provide alternative ways of thinking about the same issues.

Non-verbal tasks

Non-verbal tasks are a powerful technique that should not be overlooked by the MFT clinician. Examples range from more solitary activities such as drawing, writing or creating art/images to very active and dynamic activities such as the family sculpt. Non-verbal activities are a great way to promote reflection and learning in a way that might feel quite different to the treatment participants have previously experienced.

Separate groups

While MFT is a group-based treatment, this does not mean that the whole group needs to be together at all times. In fact, it will be important to separate the whole group into subgroups throughout the treatment. In subdividing a whole group, facilitators should be mindful that some parents or carers may not conform to stereotypical mother/father parenting roles and so separating into subgroups for the purpose of a task should involve a collaborative decision about where best a carer feels they might fit with any of the subgroups depending on their role in the child's life. A typical way to separate the group might be to break off into young people, siblings, mothers and fathers, or simply adult carers and all young people. While there is no right way to separate the groups, it is important to be intentional about how it is done and to ensure that individuals feel that

Theory, structure and techniques

their subgroup is appropriate to them and their caregiving role. Separating into groups allows people who share a similarity (or difference) to be able to have a close, more intimate conversation, allowing for greater mentalizing, understanding and validation. Earlier on in MFT, conversations might need to be closely monitored; however, later on in the treatment it can and should be less orchestrated/directed. This will allow the participants to own the experience as well as build support and solidarity. Another typical reason to separate into smaller groups is when facilitators want to purposefully have a more private conversation with one smaller group of participants. For example, it is usually important to have a separate sibling group early in treatment to ensure siblings feel important, valued, understood and heard. Similarly, separate time with parents is often needed to discuss food and eating difficulties. This has two purposes, 1) to allow parents to talk more freely away from their young person, but also 2) to send the message to the young people that parents work together and need to make decisions that young people might not be involved in.

Chapter 9: MFT meals

Meals are an important part of the MFT process and a powerful way of helping young people and their families in a very practical manner at one of the most difficult times of the day. It is also a good opportunity for young people and their parents to learn practical tips, in real time, from each other. The meals in MFT are different to the family meal session used in FT-AN. Most marked in difference is the fact that during MFT there are multiple opportunities to intervene, problem-solve, experiment and introduce flexibility. Clinicians can choose between being relatively hands-off to directly coaching parents with the other families present and observing. Having other staff members around means that clinicians can lean on each other as a resource in supporting families.

The purpose of MFT meals is multifactorial. Firstly, the mealtimes allow for assessment and observation by staff, young people and family members alike, observing what everyone is eating and the way in which meals are managed. It is noticeable that when the mealtime commences, everyone in the room is casting a very curious eye as to what others are eating. This brings new ideas about food amounts and variety, as well as new perspectives on people's behaviours around meals. There are also opportunities for parental discussions concerning how they manage the task of supporting meals, the way distress is managed, the types of conversations people are having, and the way problems are resolved.

In addition to the assessment information gathered, the MFT meals also provide space for very brief therapeutic interventions. They may take many forms, such as, concise psychoeducation about anxiety at mealtimes, role modelling, direct coaching, trying out a new skill learnt in the group, and supporting others who are struggling with the same difficulties. The brief therapeutic interventions focused on more effective ways that parents can manage their child's mealtimes will be discussed and explained in more detail in parents' groups during the initial four-day MFT workshop. Again, this will be initially led by the MFT team, but often extends out to other parents, young people and/or siblings in due course. Overall, MFT meals are a very powerful tool in normalising the difficulties families face, while enabling clinicians to join with the families and more fully understand the extent of their suffering.

Practical aspects of the meals
During MFT young people and their families eat together as a large group; a morning snack, lunch and an afternoon snack on each day of the MFT. Families are asked to bring their own food for all members of their families. This is important to emphasise in all communication leading up to the group, as this is often a source of high anxiety for parents and young people attending.

Theory, structure and techniques

A place to store, reheat and prepare meals will need to be available, as well as utensils to eat with. It is also important to make tea, coffee and some snacks available (e.g. biscuits, fruit, nibbles) for all participants (including staff), which can also be offered as extra food if people have not self-catered enough.

If at all possible, the dining area should be separate from the main MFT group room. Having two different spaces for eating and group work is extremely useful, as it allows breaks and transition from one highly emotionally charged setting to another highly emotionally charged setting. Breaks in between can help through distraction, time out, less charged and more soothing interactions with the reduction of distress, which can promote better containment of the group.

During the MFT meals, the team should arrange for two to three families to sit around one table. In other words, if possible, not all families attending MFT are seated around one large table, but the dining area consists of a number of smaller tables shared by several families.

It may also be worthwhile ensuring that there is a separate room or space that a young person and family can use, supported by a staff member, if a meal becomes particularly difficult. This might include having games and distraction/fidget toys on hand that families can use to try and help have a new experience at mealtimes if needed or to use after the meal as a distraction.

Expectations around mealtimes

It is important to set clear and specific expectations around mealtimes from the outset. As mealtimes are often a time during the day that raises everyone's anxiety, it is vital to provide structure and guidance to participants in a warm, containing manner.

This manner needs to be evident from the first discussions between the family and their therapist or MFT team in their preparation to attend the group. Information given to families include that meals take place at roughly the same time each day, which is also outlined to participants at the start of each day. The rough time limits for each meal are communicated to families by staff at the beginning of the meal. It is crucial that right from the start of treatment, the MFT team emphasises that meals are another activity in the treatment, not a break from the group. Families are informed that a short break is scheduled after meals on the condition that the lunch or snack is completed within the expected time, or as soon as they have been completed. Practical preparations for MFT mealtimes start at the introductory afternoon when families are informed that everyone is expected to eat together, and that everyone eats what is brought by their family.

Lastly, it is important to emphasise to families that staff will walk around tables and approach families during mealtimes. Staff will be clear that they will visit everyone and that their presence is not a sign that someone is doing something wrong, rather it is an offer of support. MFT lead facilitators need to make sure that every member of the MFT team also understands what is expected from them during the mealtime.

The role of the MFT team during mealtimes

Staff members have multiple roles to navigate during mealtimes. It is not a rest time for anyone – staff and participants alike. The three key staff roles are:

1. Assess/observe
2. Intervene (educate, coach and support)
3. Reflect

Firstly, it is important to ensure that staff are visiting each family to get an understanding of what each family has brought in order to determine whether, a) meals meet the nutritional requirements for their YP with the eating disorder, and b) that the content of each meal is actively working towards recovery. The aim is for the young person to have a balanced meal without avoiding any food group and for parents not to avoid challenging the food restriction posed by anorexic cognitions or potential conflict around restrictive food intake. Early on in MFT, staff will merely note these things and might not intervene, whereas this may change as the treatment continues, the families become more engaged, and as their knowledge increases.

Staff may take a more active role as well, in providing psychoeducation, direct coaching or problem-solving if necessary. The therapist's role in MFT is usually to step in and out, to offer brief prompts or time-outs, and then let the families practise new behaviours or skills. This may require several visits to a table or to a family, each time assessing how the previous strategy and problem-solving worked and then initiate further problem-solving to keep moving forward. Therapists will guide these brief conversations using the principles of FT-AN; namely, parents presenting working together, remaining firm in the face of young people trying to negotiate their way out of finishing the meal served by their parents, and presenting food in a warm, calm, supportive but firm manner. The brief interventions during the meal with individual families can be supplemented by more general discussions with the whole group, for instance about the nature of anxiety and how it can spike before, during and potentially after meals. This will help families feel better able to use skills learnt in more targeted ways. "Foster family" meals where the young person eats with other parents (see pp. 55 and 57) is an important learning experience for both the young person and parents.

Remember, there are three meals during every day of MFT, so there is plenty of opportunity to intervene or try things out. Importantly, this means that there is no need to support young people and parents to do every meal "perfectly". Clinicians will need to consider how long the group has been running for, the families' level of engagement, their level of resources as well as those of the MFT team. This will help the team determine whether to support parents to stay firm around a certain boundary that helps the young person to eat more than previously or to make sure that the young person completely finishes their meals. Helping young people to substantially increase food intake might suffice as an initial goal in the early days of MFT.

Only the lead therapists should be present to support families through the early snacks and lunches. As the group progresses, snack times can be an opportunity for both lead therapists and helpers to mingle and have some "social" conversations with families.

Mealtime clinician map
See Quick Reference Box 9.1 for a clinician map explaining how to work through the three main tasks of meal support: observation, intervention and reflection. The three steps (observe, intervene, reflect) are outlined in the map.

For the majority of families, the changes in mealtime behaviours and interactions happen visibly during the first few days of the group. Some families remain stuck initially but observing the progress of others and the support from other families and facilitators will generally help them to move on as well.

"Foster" family lunch
Families that include a member with anorexia nervosa invariably develop fixed patterns of interaction around meals that generally become increasingly rigid over time. While the

Theory, structure and techniques

Quick Reference Box 9.1 **Mealtime clinician map**

Quick Reference Box: Mealtime clinician map	
STEP 1: Observe	
Staff role	*Key areas*
Look for: - Food volume - Food variety - Eating behaviours - Family responses and tone of voice - Strategies employed by parents	Identify: - Unclear expectations from parents - Parents not united - Avoidance - Negotiation - Over talking - Criticism - Over focus on food (e.g. no conversation about anything else) - Under focus on food (e.g. parents distracted) - Parents expecting too much too soon
STEP 2: Intervene and support	
Staff role	*Key areas*

Step-by-step coaching guide:
1. Check in
2. Praise effort
3. Prompt reflection on what is happening
4. Make suggestion/ give advice
5. Expect change
6. Move away
7. Check back in
	Coaching targets:
	- What is parent's "bottom line"?
	  o Is it realistic, do they need support to make appropriate changes?
	- Provide psychoeducation around:
	  o Stage of recovery and mealtime expectations?
	  o Validation/attunement
	  o Consistency and parental unification
	  o The role of preparing a young person for a meal vs surprises at mealtimes
	  o Current level of anxiety and the role of distraction
	- Assess young person's motivation and support them to save face/"give in gracefully"
	  o What's in it for them?
	  o Use time frames to help
	  o Expect maturity using verbal and non-verbal techniques
	  o Rewards and consequences
	Use milieu
	  o Be strategic about where families sit
	  o Use upcoming activities to motivate – positively use the peer pressure of the novel context

STEP 3: Observe and Reflect	
Staff role	*Key areas*
Assess via questioning or behaviour: - parent and young person's ability not to dwell on the experience of mealtimes - family's ability to incorporate changes into future meals/ generalise new skills and knowledge	Assess timing of reflection: - Most people will not want to reflect on a meal straight afterwards. Some people will prefer just to keep moving on with the day and to leave it behind - Give it space and come back to it if young person or family are struggling – you can always come back to it Some key questions for mealtime reflections: - Did the meal seem different to previous ones to anyone in the family? - Might the meal have gone differently at home? - Why might it have been different here? - What were you doing as parents that made a difference? - What felt different for you (to young person) about the way the meals went? Would you like more of that? Would that be helpful?

mealtimes feel difficult for everyone, their predictability offers a degree of containment and makes change all the more difficult. The foster family lunch, which generally takes place on day two of the four-day MFT workshop, provides an experience of a meal where no one can rely on their usual interactional pattern of behaviour. The meal is set up very much in the same way as described on p. 54, except that no one is sitting with their own family members. Parents will often report, unsurprisingly, that feeding another child is entirely different to feeding their own; they are more likely to try things they no longer feel able to with their own child. Because the young people are for the most part fairly compliant when with adults other than their own parents, they will often respond very well to the encouragement of another parent. Parents can experience this task as highly positive where they regain a sense of efficacy and competence. Young people all know that their parents are not far away, and they are also in the company of other young people going through the same thing. Often, contrary to their expectations, the foster family groups become more relaxed and even though the foster parents encourage the young person to eat, the focus is less on food and more on other conversations.

When this exercise is introduced there is a clear sense of fear and anxiety in both parents and young people; however, it is usually one of the most encouraging and helpful exercises in relation to group cohesion and trust. The therapists reassure the group that they will be around and that they will support them again with the lunchtime task.

Chapter 10: Effectively managing and containing the group process

With a large group of young people and families who are all struggling it is important that facilitators keep a close eye on group process and the dynamics in the room. It is important that facilitators keep the individuals, their families, the group and the wider context in which the group exists in mind at any one time. Multiple inter- as well as intra-family processes will likely be occurring simultaneously, just as there will be dynamics within the MFT staff team. The most obvious markers of group process to be closely monitored will be the level of affect in the room and the level of engagement for individuals, families and the group as a whole. These will give facilitators a clear idea about whether participants are able to connect with the material, are able to process it and whether they feel safe enough to do so. Learning is unlikely to occur if, either engagement appears low or affect in the room is incongruent to the task. Other dynamics to be mindful of are specific alliances and/or conflicts.

Containing the group and managing affect

The level of affect will and should change across each day and MFT as a whole. Participants should be experiencing a range of emotions and different intensities, expressing them in appropriate ways and being supported by the group accordingly to process and understand them. Nevertheless, there will be times when the affect in the room feels overwhelming. This could be for many reasons, such as a participant remembering and experiencing something painful, or understanding someone else's pain in a new way, or it could be due to a relationship rupture within the group or with members of the MFT team.

High levels of affect in the room might be uncontaining for the group and a sign that particular members do not feel contained. It might also mean participants are unable to process the intensity of their emotions, mentalize and/or reflect on what is happening. On the other hand, too little affect might indicate the group is unengaged or that there is not enough cohesion. This is also a marker that participants might not feel safe enough to be vulnerable in front of others. Either way, it is important to ensure the affect in the room matches the task at hand. Any incongruences in the level of affect with the group content and processes should be monitored closely and managed as outlined in this chapter.

Managing high affect

It is likely that there will be times during MFT when individuals or groups of people will become upset. This might happen for all sorts of reasons and should not be shied away

Effectively managing the group process

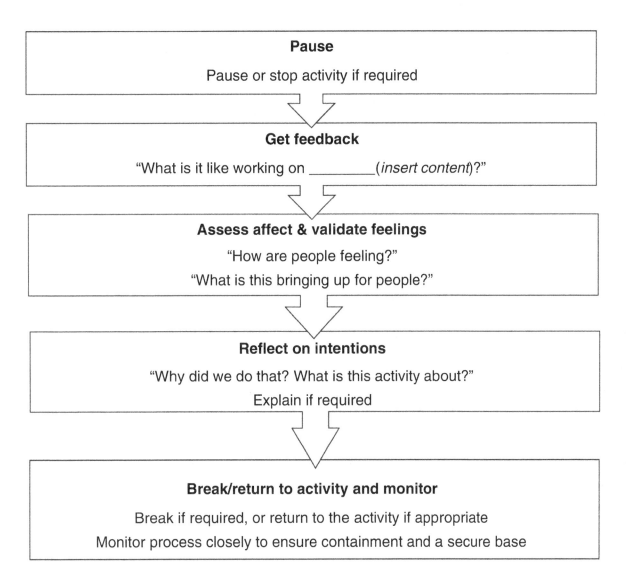

10.1

Steps to managing high affect in the group

from. On the contrary, the group will hopefully become a safe enough space for people to express and process difficult or new emotions. While high affect itself should not be shied away from, maintaining safety is one of, if not *the* most, important task of the facilitators. If high affect is overwhelmingly threatening and/or uncontaining, facilitators will need to address this quickly and effectively.

The first step is to pause whatever is happening (see Figure 10.1). This will slow down the pace and allow time for processing. In some instances, the pause may be very brief, simply to check if an individual is finding an activity too distressing or is OK to continue. The simple act of checking may provide sufficient containment for the individual as well as the group and the activity can continue. The pace can then be addressed as needed. If not, further steps are needed and feedback from the group is required to try to determine which part of the activity or conversation was difficult. Then pause and attempt to identify the trigger for the intense emotions, validate feelings and allow time for the group members to process and regulate their emotions. If this is not enough to reduce an unhelpful level of emotion in the room, facilitators need to address this directly and ask for feedback

Theory, structure and techniques

on how people are feeling. This will bring together mentalizing capacities of all group members and allow the group to process something difficult together. If this cannot be resolved through discussion of content or affect, the final step is to ask the group or particular group member to reflect on the intentions behind the activity. If the group is struggling to identify the intention, staff will need to explain the intentions behind the activity directly to the group to ensure safety and engagement.

For example, when facilitating the internalised other activity, it might be important to more explicitly explain why the task is relevant, rather than be too reflective. This can then be used to facilitate a conversation (at a later time) about how intentions do not always match with the effects our behaviour may have on others. Reflecting on intentions behind the activity is usually only required if high affect is the result of a relationship rupture. Once these steps have been followed, let the group have a break if needed or return to the activity if appropriate. Close monitoring of affect will be important thereafter.

Steps to managing high affect in the group

The steps in Figure 10.1 can be used regardless of whether an individual, family or the wider group seemingly appear uncontained. In the case of an individual or a small group appearing uncontained, facilitators might use the steps in Figure 10.1 separately to the group. This might occur either at the first appropriate break or, if it cannot wait, then a staff member can quietly take the individual(s) aside to offer support in a breakout space. However, prevailing high affect in the group with shared feeling of discomfort is best addressed in the context of a group process. It is worth remembering that this is only to be used if the group is/feels/appears uncontained and there is a concern that the high affect will lead to a rupture in engagement. High affect itself is not necessarily damaging or dangerous for the group's development.

Clinical example

Lead facilitators noticed that several families in a MFT group were consistently struggling with flexibility around food choices and amounts and created, in a rushed manner, a new activity during breaktime designed to help parents introduce some changes to the afternoon MFT meal with the support of the group. However, they provided very little introduction or rationale for the activity and some parents quickly became overwhelmed with the task and expressed anger and upset with facilitators. The tension in the group became palpable. After facilitators immediately paused the activity and followed the steps outlined in Figure 10.1, it became clear that more discussion about the intentions behind the activity and the observations facilitators had made about rigidity linked with mealtimes were needed. The shared parental perception was that facilitators were asking too much of them and were being unfair. This pause then provided the disengaged parents, as well as the other parents, space to say that they felt very overwhelmed at the moment due to anorexia nervosa as well as other external factors that had not been shared with the group. The task ended with a very helpful discussion about ensuring parental capacity and wellbeing is taken into account during the recovery process and how to balance this with the needs of the young person.

Managing low affect or engagement

Just as high affect is important to contain, low affect or disengagement in a task is important to monitor. Low affect or disengagement can be a sign of many things. There are two main reasons for lack of engagement and flat affect in MFT:

1. The MFT team and participants are lacking connection because the content of activities that facilitators initiate is perceived as irrelevant by the group members. Facilitators are not "hitting the spot", addressing the tension and preoccupation of group members that are meaningful to them, leaving them disinterested and bored. The group members appear disengaged, energy in the group is low, not much interaction is happening. The prevailing thoughts and feelings in group members and facilitators might be "we are wasting our time", "they are missing the point", "this is going nowhere".
2. Low engagement can also be a consequence of a lack of group cohesion, either because it was never established or because a rupture with the MFT team has occurred. Ruptures between the MFT team and the group members happen if the group members share the belief that the team or one of the lead facilitators have been lacking empathy, invalidating, uncontaining and have not secured group safety. This can open up the potential for destructive interactions, which are painful for one or more group participants. Lack of trust in facilitators or the MFT team may result in participants feeling threatened, resentful and defensive, and avoiding interaction with each other or with the team.

There will always be times when some people are quieter or appear less engaged. This is not necessarily a problem and can be ignored or managed with a brief check-in most of the time. However, if this becomes persistent; if it is spreading to multiple group members and/or if it appears to be leading to disengagement, then it needs to be managed directly. In order to do so, firstly pause the activity and label whatever is happening in a warm tone (see Figure 10.2). Then move quickly to getting some feedback on the activity, understanding any barriers and reflect on what might not feel quite right. Only when facilitators understand and validate what has been the obstacle for the group to engage in a task, can they then turn to problem-solving and modifying the task if appropriate. If low engagement, disinterest or resentment persists, invite reflections about the intentions behind the current task and explain your own intentions if required. The conversation can then shift to the future if needed and whether the content of the activity might be relevant in the future, if not now. Once the participants are able to return to the task, step back and let the group continue the work while closely monitoring the affect to ensure that low affect does not persist.

Clinical examples
Therapeutic alliance rupture in the previous activity
In the preceding activity, therapists placed young people in a fishbowl to feedback after lunch together on the first day of MFT when group cohesion was not yet established. Young people found the activity extremely unpleasant and became visibly distressed during the activity, which left parents feeling that the MFT team was subjecting the young people to unnecessary discomfort. When the next activity was initiated (e.g. young people's feedback on portraits of anorexia), the young people were not willing to present their work, and parents remained very quiet, avoiding asking them any questions about their portraits that might cause distress.

Initiating an irrelevant theme or activity
On the second follow-up day, the MFT team did not meet before the group and did not obtain any feedback from the individual therapist about the young people's progress

Theory, structure and techniques

since the last follow-up day. In a rush they decided to introduce activities exploring their journeys through the illness, unaware that motivation for recovery was very low in some young people and that some of them had meanwhile exhibited quite challenging acting-out behaviours.

Steps to increasing engagement and/or managing low affect in the group

---

Pause and label process

"I'm noticing _____ (*insert process*). Is anyone else noticing that?"

⬇

Understand barriers and reflect

"I wonder what's happening for the group?"
"I wonder what's stopping the group from participating in the task?"
"What is it like for people doing the task?"

⬇

Problem-solve

"What would make the task more relevant/useful/meaningful to you/your family?"
"Is this something that is needed for recovery?"

⬇

Reflect on intentions

"Why might we be doing this activity?"
Explain if required
Assess motivation
Revisit problem-solving if need be
Facilitators may want to move to new task based on feedback from the group

⬇

Monitor

Keep a close eye on process to ensure engagement returns
Encourage open expression of emotion and concerns

10.2

Steps to increasing engagement and low level of affect in the group

When group process is not enough

Despite the best efforts of the MFT team, there will be times when an individual or family requires more than what can be managed in the group discussions or via side conversations during an activity. If this is the case staff will need to take one or more people aside at the end of the day for a longer discussion. The aim of the discussions post group time is to improve engagement, understand concerns, validate and provide any private feedback that isn't appropriate in the wider group context and then plan accordingly. These discussions should not be therapy sessions and should be as brief and infrequent as possible. Only use them if the issue(s) cannot be managed during the MFT day.

Chapter 11: MFT troubleshooting and managing risk

Risk management

Physical and psychological safety as well as any risk-management plans required are important to have in place prior to MFT starting. It is typically the responsibility of the clinician working with an individual family to assess for and manage any risk. This should include a thorough medical review to ensure physical stability as well as a psychosocial assessment of any other risks to self or others, such as self-harm, aggression or suicide. If any risks have been identified the individual clinician needs to establish risk-management plans that are then communicated to the MFT team. It might also be appropriate for one of the MFT facilitators to join one of these sessions to ensure a thorough handover of any risk issues.

If a risk issue arises during MFT, facilitators need to be ready to manage the risk appropriately. Some examples of risks that may occur include, not eating when very underweight, disclosing self-harm or suicidal ideation and verbal or physical violence. This may happen while at MFT, or in the evening or morning immediately before or after MFT.

Essentially, risk should be managed according to local policies and procedures with the additional step of considering the impact on the wider group. If risk has been identified while offsite, this can usually be managed separate to the group with the individual and their family. However, if a risk is identified *during* MFT there will need to be closer consideration of its impact on the group.

Practically, once a risk is identified at least one staff member will need to make this their focus while other staff manage the group. Individual risk should be managed separate to the group using the family's available resources and in accordance with local policies and procedures. Depending on each young person's interest and needs, facilitators should support parents to demonstrate a range of responses from having firm boundaries to acknowledging that at other instances being flexible might be more important. Ideally any risk will be managed swiftly, and all participants can return to the group with a break if needed.

The team member left with the wider group will carry on with the day as planned. The group anxiety is best managed by staying calm and authoritative while allowing the discussion of any resulting distress appropriately when needed.

Once the identified risk has been managed, it can be processed, and problem-solved in the group. It might be the case that a member of the group needs to leave the group (e.g. for an inpatient admission), or to apologise to another group member or the group (e.g. verbal or physical aggression). Should something like this happen it will be important to reflect, and problem-solve first with the people involved and then bring it to the group as a whole to ensure group engagement in the process. Some examples of creative resolutions include writing a letter or meeting up with members outside of the organised MFT days to say goodbye if a group member has left suddenly.

Troubleshooting for other scenarios

Here is a list of some more common scenarios that can be difficult to manage in MFT. The recommendations are only suggestions. The most effective way to troubleshoot any scenario during MFT will be to have a clear formulation, which considers the young person, their family, the group as a whole and the wider cultural system. Having regular and structured meetings as the MFT team will ensure this is in place.

The MFT team will need to consider several things in order to know how to respond to each scenario. Things to consider include:

- The individual's level of engagement
- Level of known risk and distress
- Phase of treatment
- Role in the family (young person, parent, sibling)

If young person refuses to speak or take part in an activity

Everybody has the right to plead the fifth amendment in the group. Silence from any person does not necessarily need to be directly addressed. Facilitators should decide whether giving the silent person more focus or less focus will be helpful. If the MFT team decide that less focus would be useful, they can consider using non-verbal activities, approaching the individual during less formal times/breaks, or using foster family activities to try and encourage participation. If more focus is required, staff may want to use their physical proximity to sit closer to the individual, or to gently direct non-threatening questions their way. Facilitators may also need to judge if the behaviour is part of an ongoing family dynamic and address this accordingly.

Managing activities when the activity relies on participation in front of the whole group

A number of the MFT activities (especially the family sculpt, p. 94, and role reversal meal, p. 90) rely on inviting a young person or parent to step up in front of the group and act out a scenario. This more often than not goes very well, and people participate without difficulty; however, at times there is reluctance that the facilitators need to manage. The young person is more often reluctant to participate than a parent. Difficulty can occur in two parts of the process. The first is in initiating the activity. The second occurs when the participant freezes during the activity. It is important to note that both scenarios are best managed proactively before the activity starts. Facilitators should choose a participant they think can cope with the exposure and have a secondary choice of participant in mind. They should *not* start with an open-ended invitation such as *"who would like to join me for the next task"* as this will likely lead to no one volunteering. The facilitator should use physical proximity to help the chosen participant feel safe and more able to say yes to taking part. The facilitator should move towards the participant as they request their help and have a clear statement prepared, which describes what they are going to ask them to do. The facilitator should also reassure the participant that they will be there to help them get started. As the activity commences it is important for the facilitator to keep up the momentum by remaining in close proximity and affirming

Theory, structure and techniques

that the participant is doing a good job. If it is difficult to get the chosen participant to stand up and join (despite the preparation described above) one can try to reassure them by explaining that they will get support at each step of the activity. The facilitator might use their engagement to apply some positive pressure. If that does not work, it is best not to persist and move onto the back-up choice. If the activity involves more than one person, it is possible to ask the person who refused if they would like to join in later in the activity once it has started. It is important to let someone refuse without appearing stressed or terrified in order to maintain the containment of the group. On rare occasions it may be better to abandon an activity rather than getting into escalating an increasingly tense situation. It is important that the facilitator does this in a way that isn't defensive but acknowledges that they made a misjudgement:

> *I think we probably got it wrong when planning this activity for today and asking xxxx to take a lead. I know that this is an activity that generally gets very positive feedback from most families, but we know that even the most positively rated activities don't work for every family. I think we should explain what the activity would have consisted of and what people generally say they learned from it.*

The therapists need to be clear in their own mind that this is not a roundabout way of getting someone to agree to take on the task. The aim of the discussion is to re-engage the families and this requires being open and talking about the therapists' dilemma when asking people to do things that are beyond what they feel comfortable with. They may explain that sometimes they will make the wrong call and push too hard, or at the wrong time, and at other times they may back off too much. The message should be – getting it wrong is OK as long as you listen to feedback.

If a participant freezes during an activity, then reinforce that they are doing well with a difficult task. Provide a way forward for them that allows them to gracefully keep participating. For example, empathise with the task or ask them to try your suggestion or give them the space to think by slowing the activity down a bit so the freezing seems more part of what is required. For an activity like the meal role play then bringing a second participant in to support them so they work in a team may be the best way to help the activity progress.

A final scenario in terms of troubleshooting is to remember that at times activities can draw out strong emotions or reactions in those watching (as described in the section on Managing high affect on pp. 58–60). If this occurs, you need to make a judgement about whether to continue or to stop the activity and process with the group. It is important to remember that the key issue is containing the group by remaining calm and not becoming flustered by strong emotion. Think about how you will circuit break the level of emotion and bring it back down if needed. Some examples include pausing and asking people to reflect in their families, getting the group to sit on the floor to ground themselves, or facilitating a brief mindfulness task prior to further discussion.

If someone leaves the room

Usually, immediate family members are best placed to go and support that individual. If distress or risk is high and one staff member can be spared (not lead facilitators), they should also join to support the process. If possible, the person who left the group room is always encouraged to return to the group as quickly as possible. If it feels easier, occasionally, it might be decided that the person rejoins the group at the next natural break point (e.g. at the end of an activity). Certainly, there have been situations where a family has missed an activity because, after following their child out of the room, a situation has occurred where the child has been triggered to disclose something important. So, keeping in mind both the meaning and opportunity presented by leaving the room is important.

If someone doesn't eat/finish their meal

Clinicians will need to first decide whether either flexibility or firmness is more needed at this time. This will be informed by the meals that have occurred to date, the MFT team's formulation and family interactions observed. If firmness is needed, facilitators can offer direct coaching and use available spaces away from the main dining area. A staff member should support this process either by remaining present or checking in regularly. If more flexibility is needed, staff should support problem-solving with the family to meet their current needs. The context of the missed meal is also important. For instance, a young person may refuse part of her meal on the final day of the intensive workshop, after improved eating the other days. The parents might decide that it is a test of how much they have changed their stance and ask if they can stay at the end of the day so that she can finish the meal. Supporting them in their resolve may have an important role in bringing about a shift in eating.

Parents bring a meal that is not enough or inappropriate

This will likely require direct staff intervention. Usually this would occur at the mealtime. This is one of the main reasons why staff need to check-in with each family around mealtimes. If needed, staff can take parents to the side of the room to have a short problem-solving conversation or, if appropriate, this can be done together at the table. If parents are fearful of making a change despite intervention, staff will need to decide whether firmness is required or whether food choices and volume will need to be addressed in the MFT activities that follow as a way of addressing this less formally. It will be important to consider engagement at this time.

Hostility and defensiveness

Hostility and defensiveness do occur in MFT from time to time. Small amounts of hostility or defensiveness are usually managed by not reacting to it and taking the "heat off" any individuals or families for a short period. Taking the "heat off" particular people may be enough to allow the group to continue. Facilitators may decide to approach individuals or families in the next break to discuss any difficulties. If hostility or defensiveness persists or increases, active intervention is required as this will block the group process, particularly people's ability to reflect and mentalize. How to manage this will partly depend on whether the hostility and/or defensiveness is coming from individuals or the group as a whole. If there are high levels of hostility or defensiveness in the group as a whole, following the managing high affect flowchart may help (see Figure 10.1, p. 59). The first step would always be to pause whatever it is you are doing, label that things may feel "off" or "difficult" and try to connect with what is happening for the group. Any rupture in engagement is actually a good opportunity for deepening engagement and increasing group cohesion if a repair can be successfully navigated.

When an individual or one family become very hostile or defensive, this often needs to be addressed outside of the group context, either at the next break, or by instigating a break right there and then for the whole group. This allows one facilitator to address concerns directly with the individual or the family, while other MFT team members can

Theory, structure and techniques

organise a different activity for the rest of the group. The facilitator, in their conversation, should include both listening to and validating the person's concerns, followed by some problem-solving. It is OK for the upset individual to miss a part of the group until they feel calmer when they can rejoin the group (this can be during the group or after the next break).

If this scenario occurs, it will likely have an impact on the whole group, and this will need to be carefully managed. It is also important that the MFT team keeps in mind the group cohesion and engagement throughout the process. For example, the facilitator might say – "I can see this has become very difficult. Let's pause for a moment." The focus of the discussion should not be on the behaviour of any individual but on what everyone was experiencing. "This seems like it was quite a painful exercise for quite a few people, and it would be helpful to hear what people were experiencing". This might be followed by a conversation about different ways that people might manage difficult or painful emotions. Look for a place during the day of the incident to acknowledge the difficulty before the day ends. In the group it may be as simple as saying at the end of the day's wrap up "Thank you to everyone for their participation today. I just want to acknowledge how hard discussion can be at times and that we want the group to be a safe place to express emotions". Facilitators may also decide to say goodbye to specific individuals if they think there has been a relationship rupture.

If the young people are being friendly outside of the group
This is not necessarily encouraged; however, it does occur in many formats, for example via text message, in person, video chat, social media, email etc. Contact outside the group can be beneficial and/or unhelpful depending on the group. Its impact may also change over time. This will require a direct conversation as a group as to the pros and cons of these ongoing relationships. This does not need to be a formal or long discussion but should be talked about openly and parents and young people alike should be involved in figuring out what is and what is not helpful and how best to work together to ensure it is helpful. If deemed unhelpful, direct intervention by parents is encouraged and can be problem-solved in the group together if need be (usually separate to the young people). This discussion can and should be revisited on an ongoing basis as the group unfolds.

These conversations as a group can also be extended to social media use. The young people (and parents) who attend MFT are increasingly using social media and interested in connecting with others and society more broadly in this way. As with any type of contact outside of the group, the pros and cons of these interactions need to be discussed openly and directly. Common pitfalls, such as unhelpful comparisons and competitiveness, are typically raised by participants and are important to problem-solve together as a group. If active, unhelpful social media use is identified for one or more of the participants, direct intervention is discussed. This can be done as a whole group or with individual families depending on the type of behaviour and needs of each specific group.

If competition around eating disorder symptoms arises
This is similar to the previous scenario. It will need to be addressed directly and problem-solved accordingly. Again, this does not need to be laboured or formal; however, it can be the focus of an activity if that is the need of the group. The ideal outcome of this conversation would be to problem-solve how to use positive competition around recovery to support each other.

MFT troubleshooting and managing risk

If parents meet up outside of the group

This is not usually anything that needs to be addressed directly. This does often occur, and parents find the support helpful. If the MFT team feel as though this communication is unhelpful in any way, this can be addressed in the group together.

Low attendance, particularly at follow ups

Poor attendance is usually indicative of poor engagement on some level. Factors that will impact on engagement are:

- Frequency of follow ups (are they too far apart? Are people not connecting enough?)
- High anxiety
- Strong illness presentation(s)
- High parental stress/distress
- A feeling from the group that content is not relevant/useful
- Poor group cohesion

The MFT team will need to determine which one of these factors are impacting on attendance and modify the group structure/content accordingly. Sometimes if the young people are progressing to recovery at different rates the group can feel less cohesive and thus engagement can wane. Reducing the number of follow ups is one way of finishing the group well. It is often useful to discuss these themes with the group as a whole.

Part II
MFT activities

Chapter 12: How to use activities in MFT-AN

In Part II the activities are explained in detail. These have been divided into two sections according to when they are most often used: the four-day intensive workshop or follow-up days. However, some of them can be used flexibly and/or repeated over the course of MFT, for example photocards, "speed dating", "where do we stand" or the internalised other interview. In these instances, the therapist will use the structure of the activity, but by varying the content of the activity (questions asked and topics discussed) it is possible to cover different MFT themes. The activities are grouped together according to the theme they seem to naturally fit with and are presented in an order that matches the order in which they are often delivered – from day one of the four-day intensive all the way through to the final follow-up day. As discussed throughout this manual, flexibility in choosing and facilitating activities is encouraged in accordance with the specific needs of each group.

This book includes a selection of activities that we most commonly use in MFT-AN. Once therapists are more comfortable with the MFT model, we recommend creating new activities. The therapists should develop new activities keeping in mind the suggested themes and treatment goals specific to the particular MFT-AN group they are facilitating. Some of the best activities have been created through a quick ten-minute problem-solving session during a break in the middle of an MFT day.

The descriptions of activities in Part II of this book all follow the same format. We outline their aim, setting, related theme, phase in treatment, as well as materials needed. The instructions for all activities are summarised step-by-step with an overview of the feedback process that ends each activity. Some activities include additional notes for the group facilitators and comments we received on activities from young people and parents who have previously attended MFT-AN. At the end of the book, you will also find the activities indexed by theme and format, for your reference.

All of the therapeutic techniques described in Part I (e.g. non-verbal, active, foster families etc.) can and should be applied to the activities described (see p. 47) in flexible ways. The instructions for activities should be treated as a guide rather than strict or inflexible rules to follow.

It is important to recognise that therapists will often experience anxiety when introducing, explaining and facilitating the activities described (see Table 12.1), especially when first learning MFT. One of the benefits of working within the structures described, is to provide some certainty in this early phase. Much of the families' confidence to engage in activities will come from their sense of the therapist's confidence. A good place to start the journey to becoming more flexible with implementing the activities is to start

MFT activities

Table 12.1 **Structure and timing of MFT days**

Time	Task
09:30–10:00	MFT team preparation
10:00–11:00	Intro/Opening activity
11:00–11:30	Snack + Break
11:30–13:00	Activity
13:00–13:30	Lunch
13:30–14:00	Break/MFT team discussion
14:00–15:00	Activity
15:00–15:30	Snack + Break
15:30–16:00	Closing activity
16:00–16:30	MFT team discussion/Supervision

by delivering them as described, seeing how families respond over several groups, and using that experience to evolve changes as needed for different groups and families. For assistance with how to choose activities, see the section on clinical decision making (pp. 38–39).

As a reminder, each day is structured similarly and follows the pattern shown in Table 12.1.

Most main activities will take approximately 60 to 90 minutes to complete. Beginning and ending activities typically last between 15 and 30 minutes.

Themes

Themes are important to determine prior to each MFT day. These have been discussed in Part I (p. 27) of this book alongside a guide on how to choose an appropriate theme. See Table 12.2 for an example timetable with activities and themes for each MFT day including follow-up (FU) days. This is meant as a guide only. Flexibility and experimentation are expected and required for an impactful MFT programme.

How to use activities in MFT-AN

Table 12.2 Example themes and activities for all MFT days

MFT Day	Theme	Activity 1 – opening (10:00–11:00)	Activity 2 (11:30–13:00)	Activity 3 (14:00–15:00)	Activity 4 – closing (15:30–16:00)
Day 1	Engagement/ Understanding the illness	Photo cards	**Parents**: Preparations for first MFT lunch **Young people**: Portraits of AN	Feedback on portraits of AN	One thing to take home from the day / ball pattern exercise / mindfulness
Day 2	Managing mealtimes	Sunday lunch	Mealtime role reversal role play + Foster family	Feedback on Foster families (fishbowl)	Pebble and balloon
Day 3	Impact of illness on the family and family strengths	Family sculpt	**Young people**: Make treasures **Parents**: Food discussion and check-in **Siblings**: Own experience of the illness in family	Family crest	Traps and treasures
Day 4	Looking forward	Timelines	Feedback from timelines	Toolboxes	Photocards / Note to future self
Day 5 (FU1)	Managing conflict and relationships	Headlines	Breaking the chain	Brain scans	Mindfulness – e.g. dealing with difficult emotion
Day 6 (FU2)	Flexibility and relationships	Speed dating	**Parents**: Meal planning **YP and siblings**: Care tags	Internalised other or Anorexia press conference	Reflection
Day 7 (FU3)	Managing uncertainty	Tolerating uncertainty	Speed problem solving	Motivation see-saws	Reflection / Loving kindness meditation
Day 8 (FU4)	Adolescence and independence	Family and social circles	Parents as experts in adolescents (What's old is new and what's new is old)	Family journey	Independent eating plan
Day 9 (FU5)	Reconnecting with the lifecycle	Spaghetti towers	Where do we stand	Trip down memory lane	Setting up the activity run by families on final day
Day 10 (FU6)	Endings	Photo cards	Recovery recipes	The tables have turned	Final post-it task

*This is a guide only. The MFT-AN model is flexible, so while there will be some activities that are much better suited to early or late in treatment, there is always flexibility to change things to meet the needs of the group

Chapter 13: Four-day intensive workshop: the activities

As a reminder, the first four days of MFT-AN predominantly follow and intensify the interventions and goals of FT-AN Phases I and II. The main goals and interventions in the four-day intensive workshop are:

1. Increasing motivation and insight.
2. Externalising the illness.
3. Exploring the impact of the illness on families.
4. Trying out new behaviors, eliciting new responses to symptoms of anorexia.
5. Increasing reciprocal empathy and trust.
6. Rediscovering hope and increasing motivation for recovery.
7. Enhancing skills in tolerating distress and regulating and expressing emotions.
8. Introduction to future timeframe.
9. Multi-family meals.

Ice breakers / Introduction / Opening activities
Hopes and expectations

    Aims:
        Introduce all group members
    Participants and format: Whole group together
    Related themes: Engagement
    Typical phase of treatment: Day 1 / Beginning of treatment
    Materials:
        None

Instructions for therapists

Option 1

1. Give the families five minutes to think within their family group about their hopes and expectations for attending the MFT.
2. Ask family members to introduce one another to the group. During this introduction ask family members to tell the group what their hopes and expectations are. How much or how little they focus on the illness is up to them at this point.

3. As families go through this process with their fellow participants, they may begin to hear other versions of their own hopes and expectations. This tentatively begins the process of increasing connectedness in the group and decreasing feelings of isolation. This can be a major strength of the MFT process for families, leaving family members feeling more understood in their struggles.
4. Support this process by making comments on similarities and differences. Offer encouragement to reluctant participants. This may sometimes involve asking another member of the family to help introduce a reluctant family member or using circular questions to draw out differences and similarities between family members.
5. Once all the families have introduced themselves and a list of hopes and expectations has been generated you may widen the conversation, focusing on themes that have emerged and commenting on how these issues may be addressed over the coming days and months. This might take the form of an extended conversation with one family in the presence of the group.

Option 2

1. Ask all the parents to stand up and each of them go and sit next to a young person they don't know (they can join another parent but not their own partner).
2. Having mixed young people and parents from different families, give them 10 to 15 minutes to talk to each other as a way of introducing their families. Instruct them to listen carefully to what each are saying as they will be asked to feed back to the large group what they have learned about the other families.
3. Initially encourage them to share interesting things about other people in their family (hobbies, work, what people like about them, what pets they have) and not to talk about anorexia.
4. Then ask them to talk about the hopes and expectations that other members of their family (not themselves) have for the MFT.
5. Each of them share with the MFT group things they can remember about the other people's families they have heard about.

Option 3

1. Ask each family to have five minutes to think about one funny story about their family or some time they really enjoyed spending together.
2. Ask them to feed back to the whole group.
3. Then give them another five minutes to discuss their hopes and expectations from MFT as per Option 1.

Notes

In this early phase of the MFT process the therapists are building engagement and trust with the group. From the outset it is important to bring into conversations the idea that therapists do not have all the answers. Therapists do, however, have the experience to be confident that during the process of MFT answers will emerge that are relevant for most, if not all families. The therapists necessarily adopt an expert position in relation to their experiences of other such groups and in relation to their knowledge of the illness and recovery.

MFT activities

Photo cards

Aims:
Understand the impact of the illness on the family

Participants and format: Whole group together

Related themes: Engagement

Typical phase of treatment: Day 1 / Beginning of treatment

Materials:
Photocards / images / pictures of different states, feelings, places, relationships, locations, etc.

Instructions for therapists

1. Place photo cards on the floor in the middle of the room.
2. Instruct the whole group to stand up, move around the room and look at all of the images.
3. Ask participants to select one card to represent them as a family right now. This can be done individually or as a family. Doing the task as a family will provide some sense, early on, how they go about making decisions together.
4. Most often the instruction is to choose a card that represents what things are like in the family right now. Alternatives include choosing a photo card that represents when anorexia was at its worst.
5. After everyone has chosen and the group remains standing, provide the next instruction. People are then asked to choose a card that represents the future they are heading for if things improve.
6. People then return to the circle and sit in family groups.

Feedback

Following feedback from each person / family the facilitators discuss together, as a team, what they have noticed about the journey and strengths in each family and something meaningful about where movement for each family needs to be.

Notes

This activity provides a good opportunity to understand the length of illness, how strong / severe it is and the impact. Ensure to touch upon each of these elements with each family if it does not come up spontaneously. This activity can also be repeated at different time points in MFT-AN to explore change over time (see also closing activities p. 110).

Activities for increasing motivation and insight into the illness

Portraits of anorexia

Aims:
Externalising the illness

Increasing systemic understanding / support

Young people to express themselves and articulate struggles in a different way

Participants and format: Young people only

Related themes: Engagement / Increased motivation / Increased understanding

Four-day intensive workshop: the activities

Typical phase of treatment: Day 1 / Early in treatment
Materials:
Plain / coloured paper
Coloured pens / pencils
Modelling material (e.g. plasticine)
Separate room

This exercise provides an opportunity for the young people to get to know one another and to talk about their experiences of the illness.

Instructions for therapists

1. Encourage young people to begin thinking about how they would portray anorexia.
2. Ask participants to illustrate this in whatever way makes sense for them. They may wish to write something or to make a pictorial representation, or to sculpt with modelling materials. See Figures 13.1, 13.2 and 13.3 for examples.
3. Emphasise that the usefulness of this exercise is not only in the discussion they have among themselves but also in using their portrayals as a means of increasing understanding for the whole group. It can be described as an opportunity to ensure parents or siblings understand things that have perhaps been difficult to communicate in the past.
4. Towards the end of the exercise, encourage the young people to think about how they would like to present their work to the whole group.

Feedback

The feedback of this activity will be negotiated with the young people once they have finished making their portraits. Due to potential anxiety, the activity can be debriefed in the whole group with individuals presenting or the group of young people presenting together.

Alternatively, feedback "stations" can be used. To set this up, first ask everyone to stand in separate family groups around the room without showing or discussing the task. Leave plenty of space between each family group if possible. Parents are then instructed to move in a clockwise direction and stand by the young person (and their siblings if any) who is closest. To begin feedback the young people are asked to show and describe their portrait to the parents who are now standing with them (should not be their own). Parents are instructed to listen to the young person's feedback (and their siblings if any) and be curious about their experience of anorexia and/or of the task of making the portrait of anorexia. After a few minutes, pause the activity and instruct parents to finish their conversation and move in a clockwise direction to the next young person (and siblings). Repeat until all parents have had a chance to meet with all young people, ending with their own child. Allow parents several minutes at least with each young person before moving them on, to permit enough discussion time.

Having parents finish (and not start) with their own young person can make things easier for the young people, as it provides practice at talking about something difficult with other adults before doing it with their own family. The MFT team members also need to move around attending each "station" during the task to support any young person / group as needed. Staff also need to monitor discussion and intervene if any young person engages in "pro-anorexia" talk.

MFT activities

Parents' comments about this exercise

- This visual representation, a glimpse of what happened in the past leading up to anorexia, probably made the most impact. It revealed the loneliness of the condition young people were in.
- It was good to see that the young people were aware of the very negative impact the illness was having on the family. Until that point the young person came across as selfish with no thought for the damage and hurt it was doing around them. However, this exercise does show that the young person, separated from their anorexic demon, does understand the damage being done to their family, but their anorexic demon / thoughts are so all-consuming and focused that they are trapped within their own body / mind and are powerless to stop their negative behaviour.

Young people's comments about this exercise

- Found this was helpful because I could put my thoughts onto paper
- It allowed me to explain to my mum how I feel and what it's like living with anorexia
- Other people's portraits helped my parents understand anorexia more because they explained things that I couldn't

Challenges identified by young people

- Presenting was a challenge because I felt like what I was going to say would be judged and used against me
- Presenting and explaining my work to the larger group was a challenge

Pros and cons of anorexia

Aims:
  Increase motivation and understanding
  Promote intra- and inter- family validation
  Young people bond over common experience of suffering
Participants and format: Young people and siblings
Related themes: Engagement / Increased motivation / Increased understanding
Typical phase of treatment: Day 1 / Early in treatment
Materials:
  Flip chart paper
  Pens / pencils

Instructions for therapists

1. Encourage young people's group to generate ideas on pros and cons for having and remaining unwell with anorexia.
2. Ask them to compile ideas as two columns on flip chart paper. See example on p. 84 (Figure 13.4).

Four-day intensive workshop: the activities

13.1
Portraits of anorexia: trapped

3. Encourage examination of as many areas of life as possible – family life and relationships, peer relationships, physical and mental health and engagement with the wider world etc. Note that you need to be more interventive for this group as the young people may be reluctant to engage and therefore may require some prompting and encouragement.
4. Make it clear to the young people that the work the group produces will be shared with the whole group in a feedback session, but that the young people can choose how this feedback should be done. If the young people are reluctant to feed back, you may agree with them that you will do the feedback on behalf of the group with the caveat that if the young people disagree with anything you say they should offer their own views.

Feedback

At the start of the feedback, therapists can model curiosity for the parents in asking questions and encouraging parents to do the same. Young people should be encouraged to talk about what the process of completing the task was like. It is also important to offer praise for the generosity of sharing personal information during the task, and thus taking risks.

MFT activities

13.2
Portraits of anorexia: poison

Young people's comments about this exercise

- It made me realise the bad side of anorexia and that I wasn't alone
- It illustrated to parents why we keep anorexia behaviours thriving and showed us how destructive anorexia is to life (relationships with friends, within the family, school, sport), was encouragement to get better
- Allowed parents to get a fuller understanding, helps parents relate to us

Challenges identified by young people

- Brought up more arguments as to why we should keep thin and have anorexia behaviour patterns
- Found it triggering to think about good sides of anorexia, emotionally difficult

Four-day intensive workshop: the activities

13.3
Portraits of anorexia: two faces

Letters from the future

Aims:
  Shift timeframes to think ahead and increase motivation
  Reflection on healthy and illness parts of young people and how this might change over time
Participants and format: Young people only
Related themes: Managing emotions into the future / Endings
Typical phase of treatment: Day 1 / Early in treatment
Materials:
  Pens
  Paper

MFT activities

Pros of having AN	Cons of having AN
For now: "Safety blanket" No guilt about food Something I can control Don't have to make any decisions Achievement – losing weight Achievement – Competition with others Confidence Excuses No worries Thinking about food and nutrition all the time Closer to some family Brief 'perfection' Clear goal 'weight loss' **For the future:** Your own mind set Don't have to make any decisions Company – I always have anorexia	**For now:** Losing friends Feeling cold Loss of hair Feeling dizzy Lack of energy Poor concentration and sleep Not having a normal life Tension in my family Family relationships worse Not having a social life Losing my personality Anorexia has control Loss of happiness Perception of my body **For the future:** Not growing up Not having fun Loss of freedom Losing my independence Losing respect and reputation Losing my health Losing education

13.4

Pros and cons of anorexia

Instructions for therapists

Option 1

1. Ask young people to think about their life at a chosen age (e.g. 18, 21, 25, 30 etc.). They should choose just one age.
2. Ask young people to imagine what might be happening in their life at that time. You can do a brief guided imagery here if you feel it would be helpful. Encourage young people to think about all aspects of life, for example – where they live, who they live with (e.g. partner, friends), where they work etc.
3. Ask young people then to write a letter from their future selves addressed to themselves at the age they are now. Ask them to describe their life, what had happened to the illness and their journey to recovery.

Option 2

Ask young people to write themselves two letters from the future; in one letter describing their life as somebody who had recovered from anorexia, in the other letter describing their life if they had not recovered from anorexia.

Feedback

Feedback can be in the young people's group or feedback to the whole group.

Notes

This activity can be used early on in treatment as a means of increasing motivation, or later on as way of reflecting on the process of recovery.

Writing with non-dominant hand *(adapted with permission from Hill et al., 2012)*

    Aims:

        Psychoeducation about personality traits and neurobiology

    Participants and format: Foster families (young person and parents from other families or young person with one of their parents and one parent from another family)

    Related themes: Engagement / Insight into illness / Motivation

    Typical phase of treatment: Early in treatment

    Materials:

    Paper

    Pens / pencils

This activity offers an experiential way of demonstrating that we have propensities towards certain things (e.g. writing with one hand) that are "hardwired" and the challenges faced if we need to start acting against these. It can also be used to demonstrate that trying out new things can feel frustrating and will require practise before it becomes second nature.

Instructions for therapists

1. Divide the group into foster families.
2. Ask everyone to write down the following sentence with their non-dominant hand:

   I am writing with my non-dominant hand.

3. Ask participants to show what they have written to their foster family and invite feedback about what they noticed about themselves when writing (speed of writing, how they adapted the way they were writing etc.).
4. Repeat the exercise with the following sentence:

   When trying to write with my non-dominant hand I feel _____.

5. Ask everyone to share what they have written within their foster family and invite reflections.
6. Ask one foster parent to write the following sentence, while the other foster family members continuously interrupt them with "advice" and pressure them to complete the task as neatly and as quickly as possible:

   I am doing my best to write with my non-dominant hand.

MFT activities

7. Then, ask everyone to write the following:

    If I had to write with this hand for the rest of my life I would _____.

8. Ask people to share what they have written within their foster family and invite discussion about experience of doing activity.

Feedback

Bring everyone back together as a whole group. Ask for feedback from different foster families. Provide psychoeducation about how recovery might involve having to go against urges / personality propensities and that this may feel difficult to start with but will change over time.

Activities exploring symptom management and mealtimes
Preparation for first MFT lunch

    Aims:
        Assess current level of parental knowledge
        Understand confidence and challenges faced during mealtimes
        Provide psychoeducation and support around how to manage meals
    Participants and format: Parents only
    Related themes: Managing eating disorder symptoms / Mealtimes
    Typical phase of treatment: Day 1 / Beginning of treatment
    Materials:
        Separate room

Families attending MFT will often be at different stages of recovery. For those who are in the early stages of diagnosis and treatment, the idea of eating socially can seem extremely stressful and exposing. Parents are likely to have a wide range of fears; will my child eat? Will they make a scene? Will I be judged and found wanting as a parent by professionals and other participants?

This session is an opportunity to begin talking about these fears but also to support the parents in thinking about what needs to be different for their child to move forward in their recovery. Some parents may be at a stage where eating feels like an impossibility. Others may have managed to regain some control from the illness and have arrived at a less stressful stage of supporting their child to eat.

Instructions for therapists

1. Encourage parents to think about what changes they think may need to occur with food / eating for their child to recover.
2. Turn discussion to what parents think might be possible to experiment with, in the current context of having the support of the group (professionals and other families). By facilitating an open discussion, it is possible to begin using the experiences of group members to think of alternative solutions but also to hear from other parents that there is the possibility of change.
3. Many parents are stuck at this stage with a sense of helplessness. When this seems apparent it is critical that you convey a sense of empathy with this struggle. Normalise

and validate this sense of helplessness but emphasise the risks of inaction and keeping things the same.

4. Through the process of group discussion, the parents may decide upon different options from a range of changes; some might begin to feel empowered by the group to focus on changing the speed at which their child eats or to think about what additional strengths can be harnessed when a previously uninvolved parent is encouraged to think about how they can support their partner / child. Some parents might decide they will not tolerate cutting corners and that they will try to find ways of ensuring that everything is eaten, without exception.

5. Remind parents that the facilitators will be there to provide support and suggestions and that there will be an opportunity to think together as a group about what can be learned from the experience and how to move forward to the next step.

Feedback

Facilitators may choose to summarise the discussion at the end, just before the group goes into their first lunchtime.

First MFT lunch

Instructions for therapists

1. Advise the parents that there is a fixed time for lunch; they are normally given 30 to 45 minutes to complete their meals followed by 15 to 30 minutes "downtime". Introduce that this is a good time to think about distractions after eating, especially if this has not been raised already in the pre-lunch discussion.

2. When it is time for lunch invite the families to go to a dining room. Encourage parents to keep their child away from the kitchen and to make decisions with their partner, if they have one, about how they will organise themselves during the lunchtime meal.

3. Stay mindful of the levels of parental guilt and blame that are likely to be around during these meals. Bear this in mind when asking questions and intervening at mealtimes. For example, if a parent has provided a tiny portion of food for their child you might ask

I wonder if your decision about what <child's name> should eat today was influenced by a worry that if you gave her what you know she really needs at this stage of recovery, anorexia's influence might become really strong? I'm guessing that feels really difficult for you in the presence of people you don't yet know? We are here to think together with you and your family about how these four days can be used to start challenging anorexia and the influence it has over your decisions as parents.

Is this what she would eat at home?

Is this something we need to change over these four days?

What ideas do you have about what needs to change?

What might you do differently now that both of you can work together with all our support? Would it help if you sat each side of <child's name>; that way her dad can be more involved? Who is normally around when she eats her meals? Has her dad found himself on the outside, not sure how he can help with his

MFT activities

fear of making things worse? That might be one way that anorexia makes itself stronger, by pushing other people away.

4. Remain present, moving from one family to the next, often kneeling down beside a parent or young person, gently asking questions and gently challenging fixed ideas, especially those which may allow anorexia to remain in charge around mealtimes. However, such conversations should not be a reason for eating to pause.
5. Sometimes you may need to separate families if the levels of expressed emotion (e.g. fear, distress or anger) become counter-productive. This should only be a temporary solution to manage a specific meal and is something that will need to change over the following days with the support of the therapists and the group.

Feedback *(optional)*
Feedback after the first MFT lunch is not always formally facilitated. If the first MFT lunch has been extremely hard and emotionally draining for families, lead facilitators may decide to move to the next activity without getting much or any feedback immediately after the meal. Engagement in the next activity can model that difficult emotions can pass if attention is re-directed to a new focus and new experience (see Quick Reference Box 9.1: Mealtime clinician map on p. 56).

If facilitators decide that feedback might be useful it can be facilitated in a number of ways. If the group is beginning to form some cohesion and connections, feedback can be facilitated as a whole group discussion. When the group is less formed at this early phase, the therapists may have to conduct a turn-by-turn feedback style with each family reporting back on their experience of lunch. The therapists should comment on both the struggles and successes and encourage curiosity from participants by asking questions about how they managed to do what they did; if things went less well, what will they try this evening or tomorrow? What did they do differently? Therapists may also try to facilitate connections between families at different stages of recovery. Therapists might be curious about whether families recognised struggles they have had, when observing other families. Therapists can also facilitate a discussion about what has helped and what has been unhelpful. The emphasis should be on what they have learned and not on "success" or "failure".

Sunday lunch

Aims:
Assess thinking, attitudes, and changes around food and mealtimes
Participants and format: Whole group together, working in smaller groups
Related themes: Managing eating disorder symptoms / Mealtimes
Typical stage of treatment: Day 2 / Beginning of treatment
Materials:
Enough scissors for each group
Paper glue (enough for at least one per family)
Large paper plates (two per family)
Smaller paper plates or bowls (two per family)
A selection of food magazines

The purpose of the first part of this exercise is to offer a non-threatening context in which the patient's nutritional needs can be highlighted while also addressing the way in which anorexia has most likely interfered with their food choices. This exercise illustrates that parents know what their child needs to eat for good health and can also be trusted to provide their child with a healthy, balanced diet. The second part of the exercise highlights the way in which anorexia can interfere with parental confidence and decision-making. The exercise reveals how anorexia can pull parents into traps that may block them from supporting meals effectively. This activity allows for insight, both to parents and young people, into struggles each of them face during mealtimes.

Instructions for therapists

1. Explain to the participants that this is a family task. Parents and young people initially work separately and then come together for feedback.
2. Give paper plates to parents and young people.
3. Ask parents to illustrate a family meal that they would eat all together. They can do this by using images cut from magazines, or alternatively make drawings or write the names of food on the paper plates. The meal should include as many courses as they would normally expect at a family meal. The illustrated plate should include all the things they, as parents, believe their child should be eating and drinking at such a meal. Parents usually work on this task together, unless separated and/or living in different households.
4. Ask young people to complete the same task, but that their illustration should include the things they think their parents believe they should eat at such a meal.
5. If siblings have attended, they prepare a meal of all the things they would like to eat at a celebration meal. Sometimes siblings can be encouraged in feedback from this task to talk about how meals, eating, food choices and availability have changed for them since their sibling became unwell.
6. Instruct the parents and young people not to discuss their plates with one another until it is time to feed back.
7. Give the group about half an hour to work on their plates of food and encourage families to think about the process as they carry out the task.
8. Once the task is completed the group comes back together and parents and young people are encouraged to look at the plates and compare the results. Parents and young people also feed back to the whole group, explaining what they have put on the plates and commenting on any differences they notice between them. Encourage them to talk about the process and any surprises or questions they have for one another.
9. You may also ask questions and encourage discussion between the families. Questions should focus on how they reached decisions and how these decisions may be interrupted day to day by arguments / anorexia interfering with their decision-making. Widening the conversation to connect with the previous day's lunch can be helpful in underlining the way in which anorexia can muddle their decisions about what their child needs to eat when faced with the real task.
10. You may also encourage young people to compare their plates both with their parents and with others in the group. Be alert to when anorexia is driving the conversation.

Notes

This exercise can be adjusted so that young people prepare a meal for their parents, while parents prepare a meal for their child, or the young person and parents work together to

MFT activities

prepare the meal. Young people sometimes compile plates with exaggerated amounts of food, influenced by anorexic beliefs that their parents will make them fat. Alternatively, the young person may be so influenced by anorexic cognitions that s/he has lost any sense of what a "normal" meal comprises and prepares an "anorexic" meal.

Young people's comments regarding this exercise

- Realising what my parents would like me to eat
- It allowed me to look into the future for what I will be able to achieve when I beat anorexia and reminded me of pre-anorexic life
- Was nice, broadening my range of food, good ideas, made me hungry
- I could look at foods and feel my true self coming out thinking "wow I would love that"
- Let you realise the things you have missed, wanting food without the anorexic guilt

Challenges identified by young people

- The anxiety of going through books and looking at food (was a challenge)
- Was hard to make choices, was worried about what parents would think of our meal

Mealtime role reversal

Aims:
Assess thinking, attitudes, and changes around food and mealtimes
Participants and format: Whole group together, fishbowl (see p. 49) with role play participants, followed by group discussion
Related themes: Managing eating disorder symptoms / Mealtimes
Typical phase of treatment: Day 2 / Beginning of treatment
Materials:
None

This exercise encourages an increased level of awareness for parents in their understanding of the competing motivations when their child is faced with eating. Children being able to mirror parental approaches to mealtime support, highlights to parents that their children notice the attempts they are making (usually not apparent to parents). The task can also illustrate young people's understanding of their parents' fears when they become ever more desperate to get them to eat. The therapists need to be active to ensure intensity throughout the role play.

The whole group remains together for the role reversal exercise. This activity almost always follows the Sunday Lunch activity (p. 88). They are usually separated by the morning snack or a short break. Think carefully during the break about which family to involve in this exercise. The task requires one young person and one of their parents to "switch" roles and role play an imaginary meal. Using people from the same family in the role play helps make the role play more realistic and offers an opportunity for young people to display behaviours during role play they might want their parents to use.

Four-day intensive workshop: the activities

Instructions for therapists

1. Set up the room with a small table in the middle of the circle of chairs. The young person and parent will bring their chairs to the table during this exercise.
2. Invite the identified young person to take part in the reverse role play and ask them to sit at the table.
3. Instruct the young person to choose one of their parents (if both parents attend MFT) to join them in the role play and invite the parent sit opposite the young person at the table. Occasionally, you may decide in advance which parent you want to choose, for example, if the impression of MFT team is that one of the parents was perhaps unlikely to "play ball" and participate in the role play.
4. Instruct (it is always the therapist who is in charge of the exercise) the young person that they will be playing the role of a parent in this role play and their parent will be playing the role of the young person with anorexia. Give them name labels to mark that they are exchanging roles.
5. Explain to the "role-play family" that they will briefly role play a meal together using the "plate of food" that they made in the Sunday Lunch activity (p. 88).
6. Encourage the parent in the role of a young person with anorexia to act as a young person who is finding a mealtime very difficult. Encourage the young person in the "parent" role to do whatever they feel they should to get the "child" to eat.
7. Ask them to begin the role play and allow some time for them to get started.
8. During the role play encourage and advise the "parent" that they need to keep going. As with the MFT lunch, encourage particularly helpful and thoughtful interventions by the "parents". You can "pause" the role play and problem-solve with the "parent" as necessary. Similarly provide support and remind the "young person" to remain in role if they struggle to do so.

Optional: If the young person in the parental role gets stuck, suggest that they invite another young person either to advise them or to join the role play as the other parent with the aim to help them "feed their child".

9. Around the same time, a member MFT therapy team (usually one of the observers) enters the role play in the role of anorexia (the group may not realise this is what is happening at first as it has not been discussed). The team member representing anorexia takes a low position right beside the "young person's" ear and begins talking, at first in a low but clearly audible whisper but then with more intensity. The "anorexic voice" repeats content of common anorexic cognitions (e.g. "don't eat, they want to make you fat", "you should listen to me, you should not trust them they want to make you fat") that blocks the "child" from eating and obstructs "parental" attempts to encourage young person to eat.
10. End the role play after the "parent" or "parents" have had sufficient time to try out a number of strategies. End by interrupting and explicitly asking people to come out of their roles. Ask participants to remove their name labels now.

Notes

The role of anorexia should always be taken on by a member of staff (but not lead facilitators). If the clinician who usually works with the family happens to be one of the MFT staff group, they should also not be asked to play the role of anorexia. It can be useful to have

MFT activities

the helper playing "anorexia" change their appearance for the role play (e.g. by wearing a scarf). This can make it easier for the families to stop the association of the staff member with anorexia when the task has ended (as her/his appearance returns to normal).

Young people may be reluctant to take part in this activity or become distressed during the role play. See Chapter 11 for troubleshooting if a young person is struggling to participate in an activity and Chapter 10 for managing high affect.

Feedback

Feedback typically involves two steps. Firstly, facilitators discuss the activity in a small fishbowl (a small inner circle in the middle of the group surrounded with the outer circle listening – for full description of fishbowl technique see p. 49), with those who were actively involved in the role play (including the staff member playing "anorexia"). It is emphasised that in discussion they should give feedback as themselves (see point 9. on p. 91), reflecting on the experience. Participants are asked to reflect on what seemed to help or not help, the emotional impact of different aspects of the role play, and how the parenting team worked together, if a second "parent" is invited into the role play. After this brief, smaller fishbowl discussion, role play participants rejoin the wider circle, and reflections and feedback from the rest of the MFT group members (those observing the role play) are invited.

Parents' comments about this exercise

- This exercise was a real icebreaker with the girls getting a true sense of how difficult and frustrating it was to be the parent. They could appreciate the worry the parents felt rather than just feeling nagged. It caused quite a bit of laughter generally and many of the parents recognised the situations. I got great pleasure in being the young person and giving her responses back to her ... It was very cathartic!!
- This was a very powerful exercise and the timing of it being done early in the four-day block was good. This was the first time we got a real insight into how awful this illness is and what the young people have to endure. Seeing the psychologist then playing anorexia, was very emotional, especially when they used the word "obese", this was also a word commonly used by our daughter during our many mealtime fights, so I knew the scenario was an accurate reflection. This exercise was the dawning moment to our daughter that she had the illness as she recognised the scenario and was able to contribute.

Young people's comments about this exercise

- Showed parents how persuasive anorexia becomes at mealtimes, illustrated to us (the young people) how difficult it is as a parent to overpower those images
- It allowed me to see what my parents have to go through to get me to eat and to show my mum what I go through while eating
- Challenging anorexia's persuasion and "love", learning not to need as much reassurance at mealtimes
- Hard to see the battle our parents fight at every meal

Four-day intensive workshop: the activities

Foster family lunch

Aims:
- Try out new behaviours in a safe environment
- Provide a different experience of mealtimes
- Provide an experience of a meal when there is no predictable pattern of family interaction to fall back on

Participants and format: Whole group together, separated into foster families as decided by MFT team

Related themes: Managing eating disorder symptoms / Mealtimes

Typical phase of treatment: Day 2 / Beginning of treatment

Materials:
- Food brought for lunch by young person's own parents and handed over to the "foster parents"

Anticipation of the foster family meal often generates anxiety in both young people and adults (and sometimes therapists). Therapists need to be well prepared and not be tentative when setting up the foster families. If appropriate, they may acknowledge that families are sometimes anxious about the exercise, and that the feedback afterwards is mostly very positive.

Instructions for therapists

1. In the morning team meeting at the start of the MFT day (typically Day 2 of the four-day intensive), begin by deciding which young people are going to eat with which parents. Generally, it is best to organise this in such a way that no two family members are having lunch together, i.e. that both the young people and their parents are eating apart. If any siblings are present (particularly younger ones) they may join one of their parents. The Foster family lunch is usually introduced to the group at the end of the morning and just before lunch. Parents hand over their child's food to their "foster parents" who then supervise the meal. The young people eat the food brought by their own parents (not the "foster parents").
2. While parents are encouraged to do their best, there is no explicit emphasis on eating everything; by this stage parents and young people are aware that eating enough is extremely important. Any issues concerning how much was eaten can be fed back to the relevant parents if the meal proved either problematic or successful.
3. Emphasise to the group that the purpose of the exercise is to have an opportunity to try something different.
4. Explain that the focus of the exercise is on increasing flexibility in parental attempts to feed the child and tapping into their strengths and skills, which may have become lost when faced with a long battle over time with their own child. If preferred, this explanation can be saved for the "feedback" portion of the exercise.
5. It is expected that lunch will be completed within the same timeframe as other MFT lunches.

Feedback

Feedback can take many forms. A series of fishbowls (e.g. mothers, fathers, young people, siblings etc.) can be useful here. A wider group discussion can also suffice. Feedback

MFT activities

is focused on what was different, how people managed given the "strange" situation and what helped during the task. An optional extension of the feedback session is to generate a "top ten helpful tips for mealtimes" list following the discussion. Again, this can be done as a whole group, or in smaller groups.

Parents' comments about this exercise

- Good though challenging for our daughter. As it was early on in the MFT it gave a reassurance that all families were in a similar situation and gave a sense of unity in the group. Interesting to see how our daughter watched the other girls and was aware of what everyone else ate in comparison to herself.
- This was a good way to get to know the other parents and young people in our MFT group. Although it might have been really scary for the young people, it was reassuring to see someone else's child doing the same thing as your own. It helped endorse this is a known illness / pattern of behaviour.
- This was an extremely powerful tool, to challenge the strict and bizarre food choices that the girls were adhering to, such as a certain brand of crisps or a precisely measured amount of juice. The success was probably achieved by the staff, who lingered around asking useful questions, rather than the "foster" parents, but it was enabled by the girls not sitting with their parents, away from their parents enabling comfort zone. It also gave me a chance to get to know one of the other girls in an informal way, which was useful. Perhaps adding a certain level of trust both ways that helped once we were back in a session.

Young people's comments about this exercise

- Found it hard to eat with others but liked a less formal gathering and seeing how other parents cope with anorexia
- New topics to discuss = better conversation distraction, less intimidating, the parents fussed less about the way in which we ate, their only aim was to ensure we completed the meal
- I managed to eat with people I did not know (something I have not done with anorexia) and is a huge step forward
- Different parents treat you differently and then talking distracts you from food
- Actually, a lot better than expected and enjoyed it therefore finding it easier to eat lunch
- Helpful step towards eating at school without parents, something completely different
- I couldn't say "Dad please I really don't want to eat it". I felt I had to be polite, so I had to just eat it

Activities exploring the impact of the illness on relationships over time
Family sculpt

Aims:
Understand impact of illness on relationships and family functioning
Family timeline before and during anorexia
Externalisation of the illness

Reducing parental blame and guilt

Activate optimism and hope about the future

Participants and format: Whole group together

Related themes: Impact of illness / Managing relationships

Typical phase of treatment: Day 3

Materials:

Room large enough for a fishbowl

This exercise focuses on changes in family relationships, behaviours and beliefs over time as anorexia begins to invade the family system. The family sculpt can visually display changes in closeness and distance in family relationships and in individual and family emotions and communication. This exercise can begin to interrupt the paralysing effects of anorexia whereby time is collapsed into the present and families might be struggling to connect with their prior identity. The exercise is usually most powerful if the actual completion of the sculpt is largely non-verbal and at a relatively slow pace.

Instructions for therapists

1. Start the activity sitting all together in a large circle.
2. Invite a young person from a family you have chosen for this activity into the centre of the room and tell them they are going to become a "sculptor" for this activity. Typically, one therapist will lead the exercise. The young person and family chosen for this task should be carefully considered and discussed in the MFT team meeting prior to commencing this activity.
3. Ask the "sculptor" to invite members of the group other than their family to join them in the middle of the circle to "play" their family members, including themselves.
4. Tell the "sculptor" that their task will be to physically move the people they have chosen into positions that reflect how they perceive things to be in their own family. Let them know that to create their "sculpture" they can place family members where they want in the room as well as move their arms, legs, heads, bodies etc. Family members are silent during the sculpt exercise unless asked a direct question from either the "sculptor" or facilitator.
5. In order to set the scene of the sculpt, help the "sculptor" to think back to a time before anorexia, maybe a family holiday or a special occasion when the family were together.
6. Instruct the "sculptor" to place the family members, however close or distant, in whatever pose conveys how things were in their family back then. They may pose them smiling or angry, or relaxed and chatting, whatever feels similar to how they experienced their family on that occasion when anorexia had not yet entered their lives.
7. If the "sculptor" is unsure how to start, help them by suggesting e.g.

    Often there is one family member who is very central in the family, who would that be in your family?
    What would be the best way to place the next person in the family sculpt?
    Where, how would they be looking?
    Is that the right distance, should they be closer, more distant?

8. You can slow down the pace by asking the "sculptor" to step back with you to look at the sculpt and ask if it looks right and if anything needs changing.

MFT activities

9. Move the task on by asking the "sculptor" to then think about the changes they (as sculptor) would make to the sculpture with the arrival of anorexia. Help the young person think about how the family relationships and behaviours might have changed and how this would look as a sculpture of her family.

There are a number of ways how the therapist can lead the sculpt from this point:

Option 1

1. The facilitator brings a member of the MFT team into the sculpt to represent "anorexia". The "sculptor" then positions "anorexia" into the sculpture in a way that represents their perceptions of the impact of anorexia on her family.

   Important: *The person chosen to represent "anorexia" should not be one of the co-facilitators; if the therapist who usually works with the family happens to be a member of the MFT team, they should also not take on the role of anorexia.*

2. Make a short pause so that the whole group including the young person's family can observe the "family sculpt" with anorexia now part of it.
3. Ask people representing family members in the sculpture to comment about how they feel at this point and in their allocated position in the sculpt.
4. Instruct people in the family sculpture that sometimes sculptures can move (not talk) and ask them to think about what they would do if they were able to move. Often the family responds by closing ranks around the young person and shutting out anorexia. Sometimes anorexia will be pushed out of the door. Often this task will cause high emotions in the family and in the group in general (in particular the scene in which anorexia has strong presence).
5. Optional: The therapist leading the sculpt might then instruct an additional final scenario, inviting the young person who has been the "sculptor" to sculpt the family how they hope it might be in the future once anorexia is less present in their lives.
6. End the activity at this point. It is important that the family is looked after and that whoever played the role of anorexia has an opportunity to publicly renounce the role.
7. Once it is clear that everyone has managed to achieve a sense of themselves as safe and held within the group, support full feedback from those in the role play and the whole MFT group.
8. Ask other families if they were doing their "family sculpt" how this would look like at different time points, especially before and since the anorexia had entered their family life.

Option 2

- Once the family members are in place and the "sculptor" is satisfied that this is an accurate representation of family life with anorexia currently, ask the real family members to step into the sculpt and take up the positions they have been given by the young person.
- The young person also enters the family sculpt in the position they assigned for themselves. It is important at this point to help "de-role" those taking part by thanking

them individually by name ("Jenny, thank you for being Sally's Dad, you can go back to being Jenny again").
- Talk with the family, now in the sculpt, about where they are, what's going on for them, what they notice about the changes brought about by anorexia and any surprises or differences?
- Once the family have talked from the sculpt about their observations and thoughts, invite the staff member impersonating anorexia into the room and into the middle of the family but right behind the young person.
- "Anorexia" begins speaking to the child. The staff member impersonating anorexia is persistent, tenacious and relentless.
- The family is invited to respond. The facilitator encourages the family to "unfreeze" and do whatever they think is needed to get rid of anorexia from the family and care for their child.
- This is the end of the role play. Facilitators then move to the feedback process.

Feedback

Feedback for the sculpt often has two parts. Firstly, feedback is invited from those who participated in the sculpt itself. This can be done in a fishbowl once people who participated in the sculpt have de-roled, or from their places in the wider circle. Reflections are invited around the experience of being in each particular role before, during and after anorexia was present. Questions may focus on physical proximity or distance and the impact this made, physical positioning, facial expression etc. After feedback from those who were in the sculpt itself, feedback is then sought from the wider group who were witnessing it. Sometimes it can be helpful to ask individuals to imagine how they would have made a sculpture of their family from their perspective. Facilitators emphasise that each family member may create different sculpts as they are all impacted differently.

Notes

Sometimes the real family, who are observing their child's sculpt, try to interrupt and comment on how they see things. Validate what the young person is doing by saying that this is their perspective and others will see things differently. Say that you want to hear how everybody sees things later (the sculpt is usually more powerful if any discussion is left until after the sculpt has been completed as talking during the sculpt tends to break the intensity both for those in the sculpt and for those observing).

See also Chapter 10 of this book for an example of managing affect during this role play.

Parents' comments about this exercise

- Family sculpt is, I think, the most useful task. It was so visual and really made everyone think about what anorexia had done to the whole family, how it had isolated not only the girls but siblings and parents from each other too. I liked the way in which the task was structured making the girls and parents work through gently. I didn't think for a second until then how divisive anorexia has been.
- It was a powerful and emotional visual of what life was like before anorexia, i.e. happy and doing fun family things together, to how anorexia changes the family dynamic, i.e. angry and stressed parents and siblings keeping away from the unit / the stress.

MFT activities

- Being a three-dimensional experience added a theatricality and sense of place that words couldn't match in their evocation of the emotions revealed – the physical separation of the parents and child when eating.

Young people's comments about this exercise

- It made me see what I put my sister through and how possibly she could feel about everything
- It allowed me to see the changes that go through a family before and then during anorexia
- It was helpful to see how other families have the same dynamics as my own, making us feel less alone

Challenges identified by young people
It made me feel bad about the changes my family have gone through, even though I didn't mean for this to happen

Family crest

Aims:
Understand impact of illness on relationships and family functioning
Reconnecting with family values and family identity
Activate optimism and hope about the future
Participants and format: Whole group together, families working within their family
Related themes: Impact of illness / Managing relationships
Typical phase of treatment: Day 3 / Early in treatment
Materials:
Large pieces of coloured paper
Pens
Ribbons
Feathers
Stickers
Scrap paper
Glitter glue
Glue
Scissors

Creating a family crest is designed to help families focus on their shared identity and to reconnect with their family strengths and heritage. As families often find that anorexia has diminished their sense of efficacy and identity, this exercise is a helpful tool in supporting a family discussion but also promoting family collaboration in focusing on a shared task.

Instructions for therapists

1. Provide each family with a large piece of coloured paper and materials for decorating their crest. See Figure 13.5 for example.
2. Encourage the families to produce their own family shield that includes the strengths and assets they draw upon to support their child. Allow for up to 45 minutes to

Four-day intensive workshop: the activities

complete the shield. Explain that in the midst of trying to challenge the effects of the illness it is important for families to be aware of their family values and strengths, not only in the current generation but in strengths / values from generations before them who have also faced adversity. Help families to consider what strengths have been passed down? What family characteristics are they proud of? What do they draw on as a family to get over difficult times? What do they need as a family to protect themselves and one another?

3. Alternatively, this exercise can also be done as an exercise for young people, parents and siblings in separate groups when the emphasis can be more on creating a collective shield, combining all their individual strengths and the supports around them, which can be collectively placed on a family shield of strengths.

Feedback

Feedback is given by each family to the whole group. This is usually done by each family taking turns to stand up holding their crest and explaining it to the group. Alternatively, families can stick their crest on the walls around the room. The group then moves to each crest and the respective family presents it to the group. Feedback about the content of crests as well as the process of making the crest together is invited from parents and young people.

Parents' comments about this exercise

- A good family activity to think about your family identity and to remind the young person they are a full part of the family at a time when they are being pulled towards the separation that anorexia exerts.

Young people's comments about this exercise

- It made me think of all our positives and not just the negatives and what keeps us together, something we have not done before
- We realised some of our strengths at the end and how anorexia can be beaten by your strengths

Sibling group

Aims:
- Acknowledge needs of siblings
- Provide space for sharing experiences with others
- Provide safe forum for asking difficult questions
- Providing a validating environment

Participants and format: Siblings (grouped by age), with one to two experienced therapists depending on size and variation of ages of group

Related themes: Family and individual coping / Recognition of similarities in experience

Typical phase of treatment: Day 3

Materials:
- Separate room
- Flip chart paper
- Pens
- Drawing / craft materials

MFT activities

13.5
Family crest

Mention sibling group at introductory evening to reduce anxiety about siblings attending MFT.

Plan which day works best for all siblings involved (usually Day 3 of the first four-day intensive week).

Understand age range and determine whether to run one or two groups depending on age and maturity.

Instructions for therapists

1. Have pens / paper / craft / art material ready and offer to everyone to use as they wish during the group. This may help to reduce anxiety.
2. Open with introductions and say a little bit about yourself.
3. Prompt discussion about the experience of having a sibling with anorexia. It can be helpful (particularly with young siblings) to say that it is common for siblings to have a range of thoughts and feelings (worry about their sister, wanting to help but also sometimes feeling upset or angry or feeling left out).
4. Guide conversation as much or as little as needed – often very little guidance is required.
5. Make sure that you get everyone involved in discussion.
6. Encourage quieter siblings to join discussion by asking them if they have had similar or different experiences.
7. Write down any feedback to be given to the wider group and negotiate how feedback will be structured. For example, presented by a designated person, as a group, or anonymously presented by the facilitators. Ensure feedback is provided to the wider group next time you are all together. It is important not to miss this.

Example guiding questions

What's it been like having a sibling with anorexia?
How is the family coping right now?
How do you cope personally?
Do you talk to anyone about it?
Do you need more help / support than you're getting?
Who do we need to talk to about this? What's the best way to do this?

Feedback

Depending on the age and confidence of the siblings they may welcome questions from parents and families. Therapists should sensitively manage the feedback and any resulting questions to ensure that the conversation is balanced and that any potentially critical comments are reframed or validated dependent on their content.

Validation parent exercise

Aims:
Introduce idea of validation to parents
Provide skills and opportunity to practise emotion coaching
Participants and format: Parents only
Related themes: Managing emotions / Improving relationships
Typical phase of treatment: MFT intensive week / Very early during follow-up
Materials:
Validation handout (handouts can be found at www.MCCAED.slam.nhs.uk)
Validation multiple-choice questions

MFT activities

Instructions for therapists

1. Generate discussion about validation – have parents heard of it, what do they understand it to mean, etc.
2. Provide psychoeducation on what validation is and why it is useful. Include the difference between "listening and agreeing" when it comes to anorexia.
3. Read out the multiple-choice questions to the group and lead a discussion around responses and the differences in responses.
4. Provide the handout to parents (see MCCAED.slam.nhs.uk) and work through the steps as a group.
5. Separate the group into pairs. No parent should be with their partner.
6. Role play different scenarios in pairs. One playing adolescent, the other a parent. Scenarios can be jointly decided by the group to ensure they are applicable and relevant. Example scenarios include connecting with adolescent about peer difficulties, difficulties with school, and/or young person discussing body image concerns.
7. Make sure there is time for people swap roles to ensure every parent has a chance to experience both sides of the role play.

Feedback

Focus feedback on the experience and process of the role play. Discuss any challenges with validating and how these impact on feeling connected. Feedback can then link to the process of problem solving if need be and identifying whether parents managed to resist any urges to move past validation and straight to problem solving.

Traps and treasures

    Aims:
        Understand impact of illness on relationships and family functioning
        Activate optimism and hope
    Participants and format: Whole group together
    Related themes: Promoting trust / Listening together / Working together / Having fun
    Typical phase of treatment: Day 3 / Day 4 / Early in treatment
    Materials:
        Large room (or can be outside if not too windy)
        Blindfolds (enough for one per family)
        Paper cups, which act as "traps" (about 40 to 50 depending on size of space)
        The traps and treasures (see instructions on p. 102 for how to make)
        A reel of tape to act as a start and a finish line for the course

This is a game which is usually played towards the end of Day 3. It encourages fun and playfulness (something that families often find is missing when anorexia has a strong influence) and acknowledges how hard and intense the three days have been. It also acknowledges how important it is for young people and their parents to be able to tune in to one another's voices when anorexia is competing to be heard above all else. It can also encourage co-operation, trust, and working together (competitively) towards a shared goal.

    For the less cohesive and more anxious MFT groups, facilitators might decide to use this exercise in the afternoon of the second day to promote engagement, develop trust and introduce a sense of fun.

Four-day intensive workshop: the activities

Instructions for therapists

Part 1: Making the treasures (optional)

It can be useful for the young people and siblings to make their own treasures for the game. This makes it more personal and can help generate useful discussions within families about motivation and the future. This needs to be facilitated as a separate, young person only group. If you are pressed for time, generic treasures ("sleepovers with friends", "freedom from parents", "less anxiety", etc.) can be made by staff beforehand by writing the words on coloured pieces of paper. We have a set of generic treasures on hand for use with any MFT-AN group.

To make the treasures:

1. Have pens, paper, craft material, glue etc. spread out around the room.
2. Explain that the task is thinking all about the things that move you towards recovery and things that hold you back.
3. Ask all young people to work alone to create a minimum of five treasures that apply to them.
4. Treasures can be anything that the young person finds motivating, or anything they might look forward to doing once they are further along the recovery journey.
5. Everyone is encouraged to get creative and decorate the treasures as needed with all available materials.
6. Siblings can also make their own treasures. These could be things they look forward to doing when anorexia is less present in the family.
7. Once all the young people have made their treasures, ask the young people to mark the treasures with a symbol so their parent(s) can identify them later.
8. At the end of the activity collect everyone's treasures and let them know they will be used for a "game" later (without giving too much detail).

Part 2: Playing traps and treasures

While families are having their afternoon snack, the MFT team prepare for Traps and treasures field in a separate room (see Figure 13.6). To do so:

1. Create a start and finish line (approx. five to seven metres apart) using tape. These lines need to be wide enough that all young people in the group can stand along it with a small amount of space (e.g. half a metre) between them.
2. Lay out all the treasures randomly between the start and finish lines.
3. Then add traps to the playing field. Traps can be anything (e.g. we use upside-down plastic cups) that are easy to differentiate from treasures.
   The "playing field" should be difficult to cross without stepping on the traps and treasures.
4. Once the field is prepared, bring the parents into the room and ask them to stand along the finish line.
5. Then bring in the young people and place them along the start line facing their parents with the field of traps and treasures between them.
9. Ask young people to choose one parent to be their guide across the playing field. Other parents are to support the identified guide.
10. The young people are then blindfolded and told that on the sound of the whistle, they are to walk towards their parents at the finish line picking up the treasures along the way and avoiding the traps. They are to do this blindfolded using only their parents'

MFT activities

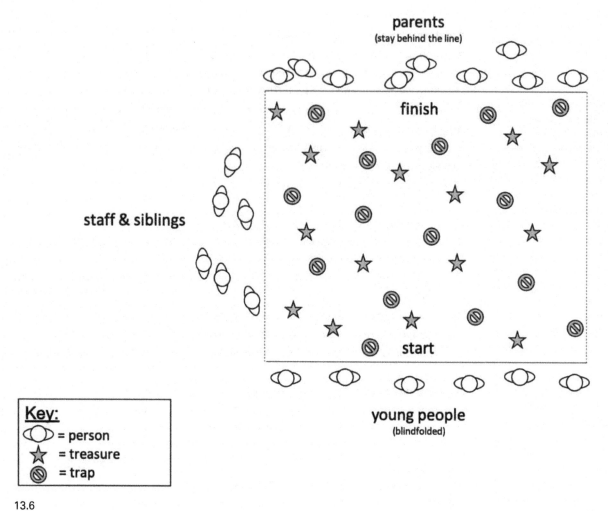

13.6
Traps and treasures layout

verbal instructions as guidance. Note: If the young people have made their own treasures, the instruction can be to only collect their own ones. If generic treasures are being used, the task is to collect as many treasures as possible before crossing the line.
11. Parents are to stay behind the finish line and are only allowed to use their voice to guide their young person.
12. If a young person touches a trap they have to be taken back to the start line. Siblings are asked to help on the sidelines offering encouragement and support.
13. Once all the young people are over the line the treasures are counted and recorded on a scoreboard. The winner gets five points, runner up three points; however, each treasure collected is worth one point, so the overall number of collected treasures can outweigh who crossed the line first.
14. Once the last young person is over the line, roles are reversed, and young people have to guide their blindfolded parent across the playing field. Again, the scores are counted and the family with the most treasures wins.

Feedback

It can be nice to feedback this sitting in a circle on the floor as a way of grounding the group from the high energy of the activity. If young people and siblings have made

Four-day intensive workshop: the activities

their own treasures, they are to collect them all before joining the circle. Young people and siblings are then invited to share their treasures with their parents. Ask the wider group for feedback about the experience of playing the game, focusing on what it was like for the young people / parents to have to trust the voice of their family member for guidance.

Parents' comments about this exercise

- This was great and "normalising", more like a family team game – we played outside, which felt more like a summer picnic and I think the girls found it easy to join in. It also helped the families relate to each other in a more normal less painful way. Obviously, it was great to get the underlying "trust" message across too.
- This was good fun and helped to lighten the mood. It was also a visual that did show how hard it is to focus on the one good voice and screen out all the other voices.

Young people's comments about this exercise

- It helped me communicate with my mum
- It was a really fun game and allowed my mum to put her trust in me (something I have to do with her while recovering)
- Was fun to play games with our parents, a nice break from all the intense therapy work that we have been doing

Where do we stand?

Aims:
Reveal level of understanding
Knowledge
Confidence
Simultaneous whole-group agreement

Participants and format: Parents only (Option 1) / Whole group together (Option 2)
Related themes: Managing relationships
Typical phase of treatment: Day 4 / Early during follow up
Materials:
Questions devised by therapists relevant to the group. Example questions can be found on p. 106.

This is an activity that lends itself nicely to being run in parallel to the young people making their traps and treasures. However, this activity can also be done with the whole group.

Initially, it was devised as a way of instigating a discussion with a group of parents based around their level of self-efficacy in supporting a child with anorexia. There is scope to ask any question that is relevant to the group at the time.

Instructions for therapists

1. Before the activity, write the words "strongly agree" on one piece of paper and "strongly disagree" on another. Stick the "strongly agree" piece on one side of the room /

MFT activities

space. Then stick the "strongly disagree" piece on the opposite side of the room / space. This creates a physical continuum between these two extremes.
2. Explain to participants that facilitators will read aloud several questions / statements during this activity and that participants need to answer each question / statement by physically placing themselves somewhere along this continuum without speaking.
3. Read aloud the first statement / question.
4. Once participants have placed themselves physically along the continuum, facilitators then approach different people and ask them to explain why they have placed themselves in that particular spot. This usually generates a wealth of discussion and opens up conversations that may have previously felt difficult to have.
5. If multiple family members are present, it can often generate interesting conversations about differences of opinion within a family.
6. For some questions facilitators may ask the group where they think the therapists would place themselves on the continuum. Typically, facilitators would then place themselves in the room / space and explain their own thinking.
7. There is usually enough time for five to six questions in a 60 to 90 minutes MFT activity slot.

Example questions:
Questions asked during this task are often slightly provocative to ensure there is a range of responses. Facilitators can aim to be playful with this.

Parents do not have the capacity to help their child overcome anorexia
Parents are to be blamed for anorexia
Although I can help my child s/he will never get better unless they get individual therapy
It is more my responsibility than my child's to bring him/her to a healthy weight
I have enough strategies to help my child recover
Being too firm is wrong because my child is experiencing enough distress
My own parental instincts are a more reliable guide for recovery of my child than any expert advice I might get from professionals
Parents cannot be seen as the solution in the treatment of anorexia until what caused it has been properly explored
My child is fully recovered right now
My communication with my parent / child has improved during treatment
Your parents/I understand and connect with what is going on for with me/ my child
We are problem-solving effectively as a family right now
Parents are currently in tune with what is going on for their child with anorexia

Notes

It is important that facilitators create their own list of questions depending on the themes and phase that the group is in when using this activity.

There is opportunity in this task to support thinking about how things change over time. Facilitators can encourage participants to rethink their answer to a particular question for the present, past and future or for the early, middle and late stages of recovery. Once a statement is answered, facilitators can invite participants to see if they would change their answer depending upon these timings.

Activities exploring looking forward and coping ahead
Family timelines

Aims:
- Encourage families to think about the future
- Motivation
- Coping ahead and using skills beyond the first four days

Participants and format:
- Whole group together, families working within their family
- Individual family therapist / care co-ordinator (if possible)

Related themes: Looking forward / Coping ahead

Typical phase of treatment: Day 4

Materials:
- Flip chart paper
- Coloured pens

Family timelines support future thinking and planning of the steps towards recovery in a systematic way. Timelines might also give parents "permission" to support important changes in relation to feeding their child or managing difficult behaviours and offers patients a visual motivator when the timeline includes enjoyable and encouraging events as well as challenging steps on the road to recovery.

Instructions for therapists

1. Instruct families to work in their family groups to start planning their next nine to twelve months. See example on p. 109 (Figure 13.7).
2. Families work on three separate timelines and map the following:

    a. First timeline: Timeline of family life

    Tell families to include on their timeline all the upcoming events they know about, e.g. family birthdays, holidays, Christmas, exams etc.

    b. Second timeline: A timeline for recovery

    Ask young people to work with their families on pinpointing when significant shifts will be made, e.g. eating independently at school, returning to doing sports, going on holiday with friends, going on a sleepover etc. If a young person has been out of school, for example, they may want to think about when it would be possible for them to return to school and to put the steps towards this on the timeline. They may want to include small steps towards regaining independence depending on the phase of treatment for that particular family.

    c. Third timeline: A timeline depicting the future if they do not recover

    This timeline might include going into hospital, remaining out of school, missing out on higher education, not getting a job etc.

Notes

Therapists and helpers will have to decide which families might need more or less support with this task. Ideally the family's therapist should join the family for this exercise. The therapist joining the family can invite them to think about those things that have maybe been

MFT activities

put on hold or seemed impossible with anorexia in control. If family holidays have been impossible, what would need to change between now and a planned holiday for them to feel more confident that they could manage this? For families who might find the task difficult, therapists should support the family to think through the steps towards achieving change in the future, possibly offering examples of how other families planned these necessary changes.

Feedback

Families are given a good amount of time to feed back their timelines to the rest of the group. Families should decide who will present the timeline to the whole group. Feedback is about all three timelines.

Parents' comments about this exercise

- This worked well for us as a group – opening up our family lives, revealing interests, hobbies, family events, holidays, and a simple ambition of returning to a more predictable life. It also helped set some real goals for the girls too, as well as the parents. By this point in the MFT it was important that the parents also had something to look forward to, something as simple as attending a family wedding.
- Young person had this up on her wall and when she was struggling, we could focus her on things that she had said she wanted to do. It gives hope to the parents that the professionals expect an improvement.

Young people's comments about this exercise

- It made me think of things to look forward to in my recovery and gave me motivation.
- This was helpful as it allowed me to realise there is a future without anorexia. How I can be able to get better and what things I would miss if I kept the illness.

Toolboxes

Aims:
 Explore coping strategies in tolerating distress
 Regulating and expressing emotions
Participants and format: Whole group together, separated into smaller groups (mothers, fathers, young people, siblings)
Related themes: Managing emotions into the future
Typical phase of treatment: Day 4 (final task)
Materials:
 Pens / pencils
 Paper
 Modelling materials
 Glue
 Ribbons and other decorative materials

Four-day intensive workshop: the activities

Timeline with recovery

By Oct	By Nov	By Dec	By Feb	By Apr	By May	By Aug	By Sept
Go back to school	**Join in**	**Trust my parents**	**Trusted to go**	**Feeling stronger**	**Able to sit exams**	**Festival!!**	**Exam results**
Lunch support and then practise choosing snacks or breakfast. Practise eating with friends out of school	Eat some cake!	Ask for help when I need it but remember I have practised and can do this	Mum and dad trust me more and I get to go on the trip!	I feel stronger and don't feel dizzy. My body is recovering	I don't spend all day thinking about food so my concentration seems to be much better and I don't panic so much or spend my whole time worrying	I can't believe this will really happen! I really hope it does if I have managed everything else	Go to 6th Form with my friends because I got the grades!

October	November	December	February	April	May–June	August	September
Finish MFT	**Brother's birthday**	**Christmas**	**School Trip**	**Family Ski Trip**	**Exams**	**Festival with friends**	**Start 6th Form**

Timeline without recovery

Stay at home, feeling too anxious	Too fearful of change, life is very unpredictable	Everyone is sad and worried all the time	Feeling weaker, waiting for a hospital bed	Ski Trip cancelled	Exams postponed for a year, losing touch with friends	Friends go to the festival without me	Can't go on to 6th Form. Feeling tired and numb, or scared, angry and guilty

13.7

Family timelines

Instructions for therapists

1. Split up into mothers, fathers and young people (and siblings if present).
5. Give same instructions to each group: tell them that in the days, weeks and months to come they might want to draw on all the tools they acquired during the four-day workshop.
2. The toolboxes they put together should include all those things that will support them and help them on the journey towards recovery. They may have some "emergency" tools or "everyday" tools, tools for themselves or tools to give to others, but all of these should be illustrated or listed in whatever way they would like.
3. Individuals then plan how to physically make their emergency toolbox at home. This might include listing items to collect once at home, identifying a place or a physical box where these items can be stored, etc.

Feedback

Once completed, the groups feed back to the main group and are encouraged to ask questions and think about tools they might have forgotten but another group included.

Notes

Group is encouraged to use the toolbox in between follow ups.

This activity provides an opportunity for increasing connections between the members of the group and recognises gender and age differences in relation to appropriate mechanisms for support.

MFT activities

Parents' comments on this exercise

- By the time we did this activity at the end of the block four days, the different groups (men, women and young people who worked in these groups) felt comfortable enough with each other and knowledgeable enough from the last four days to come up with the very practical tools which we could take home to help manage anorexia on our own.
- This was the point that the women suggested a "group email" support system which went on to be a great source of support in tough times between the various families, but also continues to be a great support even though most of us have now been discharged from the Maudsley. FYI the women are better at opening up and keeping in touch.

Closing activities for the four-day intensive workshop

Choose one of the activities listed below as a closing activity on Day 4.

Pebble and balloon

Aims:
Quickly check in with participants about key learning from the four-day workshop and applications for the future ahead

Participants and format: Whole group together

Related themes: Managing emotions into the future / Endings

Typical phase of treatment: Day 2, 3 or 4 (final task)

Materials:
Pens
Small pieces of paper (preferably two different colours – one for the pebbles and one for the balloons)

Instructions for therapists

1. Give each participant two pieces of paper, each a different colour.
2. Ask each participant to write down one thing they want to hold onto (pebble), on one piece of paper, and one thing they want to let go of or throw away (balloon), on the other.
3. Ask participants to place the pebble in their pocket and try to act upon it in the evening after the group. Participants need to bring it back to group the next MFT-AN day or follow up day.
4. Go around the circle and ask participants to one-by-one say out loud what their balloon is, then scrunch it up and place in a bin in the middle of the circle.
5. No reflection is required. The group can then end for the day.

Note to future self

Aims:
Help people to reflect on and consolidate their learning from the workshop for the future ahead

Participants and format: Whole group together, with people working individually

Related themes: Looking forward / Fostering self-reflection/ Looking forward to trying out something new

Typical phase of treatment: Day 4 (final task)

Materials:
Pens
Paper
Envelopes

Instructions for therapists

1. Provide participants with pen and paper.
2. Ask each participant to write a note to themselves that consolidates how they are feeling right now and what they feel will be important to hold onto to promote recovery.
3. Alternative: Ask participants to write a note to oneself outlining something new they want to try before the next follow up.
4. Inform them that the personal note will be sealed and provided to them on the first follow-up day.
5. Ask everyone to place their note in an envelope, seal it, and write their name on the front.
6. Collect the envelopes and store safely. Remember to bring these back to the group on the first follow-up day.

Feedback

At the next follow-up day envelopes are placed on chairs prior to participants entering the room or handed out once they have arrived. Participants are then invited to read the note quietly to themselves. Feedback can then be done in various ways. Facilitators might invite feedback in the wider group about the note and what has happened since the last MFT-AN day. Other options might be to share reflections about the personal note in a small group huddle with those around them. It is important to remind people that they are able to share as much or as little as they are comfortable doing, as this is quite a private task.

Photo cards

Aims:
Shift the timeframe to think about the four-day intensive workshop and the future ahead
Getting a record of any changes in the families' perceptions of themselves

For the basic instructions on how photo cards are used see p. 78. For the closing task, participants choose two cards. First, one that expresses their current emotions and thoughts, and a second, about how they would like things to be in the future. Following feedback from each person, the facilitators discuss together, as a reflecting team, what they have noticed about the strengths in each family and what the next step for each family might be.

Mindfulness exercises

Within MFT we aim to introduce the idea of mindfulness as a potentially useful tool for families to regulate their distress and emotions after heightened emotional arousal.

MFT activities

Typically, facilitators' guided mindfulness activity is used in MFT at the end of a day to down-regulate the affect before families go home. Some example activities include mindful breathing, safe-space visualisation, loving-kindness meditation and the ball pattern exercise below. Other than the ball pattern exercise, a comprehensive list of mindfulness exercises or instructions are not described here. There is now an abundance of resources, books, apps, video and audio recordings freely available on the internet. Facilitators are encouraged to find mindfulness activities that they connect to. There is no such thing as choosing the "right" mindfulness task. For the mindfulness to be effective, the most important thing is that facilitators only do it if they actually believe that mindfulness can be helpful and only if they are able to connect mindfully with the task in hand. As with all things MFT, it is more about the process than the activity itself.

Ball pattern exercise
Note: Instructions for the ball pattern exercise are included because it is not commonly described, not because it is the "best" mindfulness activity to use

Aims:
Down-regulate or shift group affect
Promote and model self-care
Participants and format: Whole group together / Individual groups
Related themes: Managing emotions
Typical phase of treatment: End of Day 1 / End of Day 2 / End of Day 3
Materials:
Coloured balls for throwing (four to six in total)

Instructions for therapists

1. Everyone, including all facilitators and helpers, stand in a circle.
2. The facilitator instructs everyone that a ball will be thrown around the circle in a random order.
3. The ball needs to go to every member of the group, without repeating anyone and then return to the lead facilitator.
4. Each individual chooses who to throw it to during the first round.
5. Once the ball has been thrown to every person, the order is set. Participants are asked to remember the order as this will remain for the rest of the task.
6. Participants then start throwing the ball in the same order around the group more quickly.
7. Once the group feels more confident with one ball, the lead facilitator starts to introduce a second, then a third and so on, so that multiple balls are in rotation simultaneously.

Feedback
Once the facilitator ends the task participants are asked to comment on how they found participating in the task. The discussion might include whether it was difficult / easy, whether participants' minds wandered, whether certain strategies helped them stay focused on the task, whether participants made any judgements (internal or external) etc. Facilitators may also want to discuss / comment on whether the task helped to mark the end of the day and shift affect.

Chapter 14: Follow-up days and exercises

There is flexibility within the follow-up days regarding themes and activities. The number of follow-up days can be negotiated with the group and MFT team. More follow-up days should be offered if the group is working well together and the families are connecting with the content – "a working group" in group analytic terms. The timing of follow-up days is also important to consider. Having follow-up days closer together will enhance group cohesion, whereas spaced further apart will encourage independence. The first follow-up day and the four-day intensive are a minimum of one week apart.

Follow-up day techniques

Facilitators might decide that certain exercises would work better if the young people do them in the setting of the "foster family". The "foster family" can be the same or newly formed at the follow-up.

The task would always involve the young person and "foster parents" discussing certain questions / themes set up by MFT facilitators or problem-solving particular difficulties. Foster families are used in order not to raise defences and repetition of the same vicious circle often present in extremely tense relationships between young people and their parents, and allow more flowing discussion between adolescents and adults.

Introductory activities for follow-up days
Letter from the previous day

> **Aims**:
>   Help participants reflect on the four-day workshop
> **Participants and format**: Whole group together, with people working individually
> **Related themes**: Fostering insight and learning
> **Typical phase of treatment**: Follow-up day 1
> **Materials**:
>   Letters / notes to selves written during the previous MFT day

Letters and notes written to oneself or others can be used throughout MFT in various ways. One way that can be quite powerful is to have people write a letter to themselves at the end of the four-day workshop, which they then read at the beginning of the first follow up day.

DOI: 10.4324/9781003038764-14

MFT activities

Instructions for therapists

1. The "notes to self" that were written in the previous day are awaiting each person in the group on their chair as they walk into the group.
2. Everyone is given an opportunity to read their note and reflect silently.
3. After a short amount of time, feedback into the wider team is encouraged.

Feedback

This should focus on changes since the last group and what has changed. Therapists can also invite feedback on the experience of trying out new behaviours.

Headlines

Aims:
  Feedback and update on the time since the last MFT meeting
Participants and format: Whole group together, split into family groups
Related themes: Gathering information / Fostering insight and learning / Reinforcing changes
Typical phase of treatment: Follow-up days 1, 2 or 3
Materials:
  Flip chart paper
  Pens

This task is presented as an opportunity to catch up with each other and report back on significant events; positive, light-hearted and challenging. The purpose is both an icebreaker for the group and an opportunity to begin detecting themes that have emerged over the intervening weeks of the MFT.

Instruction for therapists

1. Divide the group into parents and young people. Each group should choose an "editor" for their newspaper and as a group come up with typical "red top" headlines, which should be cryptic enough to ensure that the family or person it refers to is not immediately obvious. If possible, young people and the parent group should complete this part of the task in separate rooms.
2. Each young person and each parental couple/parent should be encouraged to come up with at least two headlines each.
3. The headlines should refer to achievements, difficulties or any family events of interest or note. Instruct both groups to put together a front page, which is then fed back to the main group with families and individuals trying to guess which headline belongs to whom.
4. Alternatively, each family can create their own family headlines and feed back to the group.

Speed dating

Aims:
  Support problem-solving in different groups to generate new ideas
Participants and format: Whole group together

Follow-up days and exercises

Related themes: Applicable to all themes
Typical phase of treatment: Follow-up days 2 or 3 onwards
Materials:
Large room

The speed dating task is designed to allow individuals in the group to interact with members that they might not usually talk to in a light and quick way.

Instructions for therapists

1. Set up the room so that the chairs are arranged in two circles, one inside the other. The chairs should be facing each other in pairs. Have the room set up in this way before people enter.
2. As people enter the room ask them to sit anywhere they like. Once everyone has sat down everyone should be facing another person in pairs.
3. Facilitators then explain that the format is speed dating. Questions will be read out loud and pairs are to discuss the answers.
4. After each questions the outer circle stands up and moves one chair clockwise meaning new pairs are generated for every question. The inner circle remain in their seats.
5. Questions will generally start quick and light, and move to more difficult.

Example questions include:

What is something I'm proud of since the last MFT day?
What I will do the day I turn 18 / what I did when I first turned 18
One challenge I faced but didn't tell anyone about since the last MFT day?
The thing I'm struggling to talk about most at the moment is ...

Feedback
General feedback is usually in the wider circle. It is not necessarily important to hear from everybody, but just to ensure the conversations are brought back to the group as a whole. If facilitators are interested in a particular topic, they could ask specifically about what people discussed for that question. Some groups may also benefit from writing ideas down from different questions on flip chart paper and putting them up on the wall as reminders of progress, positive things, changes etc.

Spaghetti towers

Aims:
For families to have a fun and enjoyable experience of working together
Participants and format: Whole group together
Related themes: Working together / Having fun
Typical phase of treatment: Anytime
Materials per family:
20 sticks of dry spaghetti
1 metre of string
1 metre of sticky tape
1 marshmallow

MFT activities

Spaghetti towers is a short activity that can be used to lighten the mood of the group or to start/end a MFT day. It is a nice way of helping a family work together and have some fun when things feel stuck or difficult.

Instructions for therapists

1. Each family is provided with the materials listed.
2. Instruct participants that they have 15 minutes to build the tallest possible tower they can using the materials provided.
3. The marshmallow must be on the top of the tower.
4. The winner will have the highest tower, measured from the ground (or tabletop) to the top of the marshmallow.

Notes

This is an activity that is used in many corporate / professional settings. Some of the participants may have done it before. It is usually a bit silly and fun, with lots of noise in the room.

Activities targeting motivation, challenging behavioural patterns and their exits, and increasing mutual understanding
Brain scan

Aims:
To help individuals mentalize and empathise with different people in the family
Participants and format: Whole group together, with people working individually
Related themes: Increased understanding / Improving communication
Typical phase of treatment: Early during follow-up
Materials:
Printouts of the brain scans (Figure 14.1). Alternatively provide blank paper and ask participants to draw the outline of the brain scan themselves using Figure 14.1 as reference.
Pens

This exercise invites individuals to try and imagine the thoughts and emotions of others. The task requires people to fill in the empty areas ("bubbles") of the "brain scan" handout (Figure 14.1) for different family members. It is a playful way of getting people to mentalize and openly discuss what is taking up the most "brain space" at the moment.

Instructions for therapists

1. Before introducing the task, facilitators need to identify whose brain to "scan" during the activity.

   a. Option 1: All participants complete a brain scan for the closest family member to their left.
   b. Option 2: One family member of your choosing.
   c. Option 3: One brain scan per family member attending the group that day.

Follow-up days and exercises

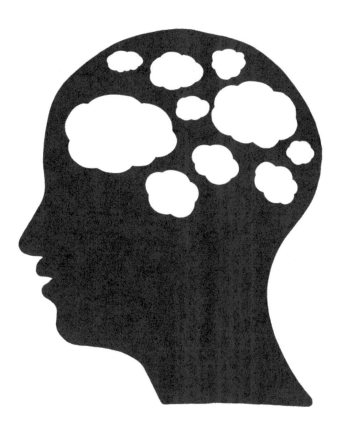

14.1
Brain scan

2. Start the exercise by asking family members to move into small circles.
3. Handout the blank "brain scan" printouts and instruct participants to fill in the blank spaces with the thoughts and feelings that they think the identified family member(s) might currently be experiencing. Ask participants to consider the size and position of different thoughts / feelings. For example, thoughts / feelings that people are most preoccupied with should take up the most space; some thoughts / feelings might be more at the "front" of the brain scan vs buried at the "back"; those that are never far from consciousness might be near the top of the brain scan, etc.
4. Then ask each participant to complete their own brain scan.
5. Move to Feedback.

Feedback

Ask participants to discuss the brain scans in family groups and then to feed back to the group. Ask them to compare and discuss what were the similarities and differences between what different family members imagined and personal brain scan. How accurate is the perception of others? What were the surprises arising from the exercise?

Notes

This can elicit surprise about how much one person can understand the other, or it can highlight gaps in people's understanding or knowledge of others.

MFT activities

Participants' comments about this exercise

- Made us focus on what our nearest and dearest were feeling and why, and which helped us to develop strategies to support them as well, i.e. a problem shared is a problem halved.

Breaking the chain

Aims:

Supporting families to break unhelpful and repetitive behavioural patterns

Using problem-solving techniques in different groups to generate alternative responses and solutions

Participants and format: Whole group together, families working within their family

Related themes: Managing conflict / Maintaining relationships

Typical phase of treatment: Early during follow-up

Materials:

Flip chart paper

Pens

This exercise is for families where distressing, aggressive or emotional incidents get out of control or keep repeating and feel stuck. Incidents can be big or small but should involve more than two family members to ensure it is relevant for the family as a whole. It should also be an incident / pattern that all agree they want to change or be different. The exercise is designed to help families work collaboratively on finding solutions and alternative responses. The emphasis is on the solutions, rather than the event itself.

Families are instructed to work together to create a detailed timeline of events, emotional reactions and thoughts that led up to and occurred directly after a difficult family interaction (see Figure 14.2 for example). For therapists familiar with the concept of chain and solution analysis, this activity is like conducting a family chain analysis.

Instructions for therapists

1. Instruct families to discuss – within the family unit – a past, distressing incident and identify one for which they would like to find alternative solutions.
2. Once an incident is identified instruct the families to write in detail what happened in the build-up to the event as well as what happened afterwards.
3. This may include what each family member had said, done, how they felt or what they thought.
4. Instruct participants to be as detailed as possible and to draw on the A3 piece of paper a chain (steps that can be visually represented in a circle) and write down on each chain link what were thoughts / feelings / actions (or lack of action) by different family members.
5. Once a detailed chain of events has been created, ask families to then generate / brainstorm alternative solutions (alternative responses by all or some family members) for each step identified that can break the chain and stop family interactions proceeding to the next link.
6. Ask families to write down the alternative solution they brainstormed at the corresponding points of the chain.

Follow-up days and exercises

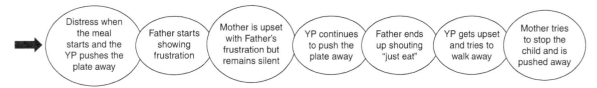

14.2
Breaking the chain example

7. Make sure participants include all family members in solutions, not just one person. Be sure to emphasise that everyone will have a role to play to reduce criticism or potential blame of one person or persons.
8. Ask participants to include solutions for after the event as well, to ensure they also focus on relationship repair when needed. For example, making an apology or spending time together once things calm down so that everyone feels like the distressing situation has ended.

Feedback

Feedback can be organised in several ways depending on what the facilitators feel is pertinent for the group of families they are working with.

Option 1: Ask families to split in pairs to look at their chains and focus particularly on the solutions / repair phase. They can consult with one another and feed back their ideas to the whole group.

Option 2: The chains are placed around the room. The whole group is divided into mothers, fathers and young people groups. The groups move around the room and talk together about the different ideas generated by the task. These groups can then feed back to the main group.

Notes

This can sometimes be a difficult task to do as families often fall into the patterns present during the argument again when doing the activity. Often staff are needed with each family to support them through the process. The focus on the activity should be on the solution at each point rather than the problem. It is also useful to specify that the start of the chain should be no further back than 24 hours before the peak of the difficulties. This will ensure the chain is focused and the suggested resolutions are relevant and appropriate.

Motivation see-saws

Aims:
Support problem-solving in different groups to generate new ideas
Participants and format: Whole group together, working in smaller groups
Related themes: Motivation / Looking forward / Managing uncertainty
Typical phase of treatment: Follow-up days 1, 2 or 3
Materials:
Flipchart paper
Pens
Sticky notes

MFT activities

This task is most often used in early follow-up days. It can acknowledge that "pros" of anorexia can persist in the minds of young people and that systems can accommodate patterns that keep anorexia going. More importantly it can build or refuel motivation to persist in the fight against anorexia even when the journey to recovery seems long.

Instructions for therapists

1. A balanced see-saw is drawn on a large piece of paper and given to each family group. A stack of sticky notelets and pens are provided.
2. Groups are first asked to write on notes the things that can tip motivation to recovery downwards and stick them on the poster paper. Examples can be given like, "It is too hard", "I'll look terrible", "No-one will notice when I'm not okay if I recover", "I can't bear another stressful dinner".
3. Secondly, participants are asked to think creatively about motivators that can help when times are hard and stick them on the poster, for example "I can concentrate better with nutrition", "I want to be independent and leave home", "A lapse is not a relapse".

Feedback

Families are then asked to present to the larger group, and to reflect on how they can use the motivators in family life.

Alternatively, rather than a group discussion, families are asked to tour the see-saws of other families and donate motivators to make sure the balance is tipped well and truly in the right direction.

Notes

The way the larger group is broken into smaller groups for this task is dependent upon the needs of the group. This can be done in families, foster families, or in groups, depending on a characteristic (e.g. mums, dads, siblings, young people). Groups may be joined by a helper.

Activities targeting building relationships, social networks and reflecting on body image

"Internalised other" interview

> **Aims:**
> Increase reciprocal empathy and trust
> Promote mentalizing
> **Participants and format**: Whole group together, separated into parents and young people
> **Related themes**: Managing relationships / Independence / Promoting empathy and understanding
> **Typical phase of treatment**: Follow-up days 1, 2 or 3
> **Materials:**
> One-way mirror (or video-link room)

"Internalised other" interviewing can be used on any of the MFT days but lends itself to sometime early in follow-up. The focus of this exercise is on increasing empathy

Follow-up days and exercises

and understanding, and encouraging perspective-taking and discussion. For many of the families attending the MFT, there may be a sense that communication and understanding has been interrupted by the illness, which causes sadness, friction, anger and / or frustration. When speaking from an "internalised other" position, it is possible to demonstrate in a safe way just how much each understands and empathises with the other. Even when people "get it wrong", the ensuing discussion can be an opportunity to enhance understanding and develop communication.

There are many ways in which this task can be set up, for example, see Instructions for therapists.

Instructions for therapists

1. If using a one-way mirror, the parents are led into the therapy room by one of the therapists while the young people, other therapist, helpers and observers remain behind the screen.
2. In both set-ups, the parents are encouraged to write their child's name on a name label and then the therapist asks them to respond to questions as if they are their child. It does not matter that there might be two parents responding from their child's perspective.
3. The therapist begins by asking questions that help the parents begin to think like their child; how old are you? Do you have any brothers and sisters, what are your parents' names? Do you have any hobbies? etc.
4. Once parents seem to be in the role of their child, the therapist can begin asking questions related to the illness, to family life now, in the past and in the future, relationships, hopes, fears, dilemmas.
5. The therapist might also want to draw out information related to particular themes that have been emerging over the course of the MFT.
6. The conversation is observed by the rest of the group and the young people are encouraged to listen carefully.

This task can be swapped around, and the young people can be interviewed as their parents (one way of beginning this in a playful way, and so encouraging quiet people to participate, can be to set up the scenario of a reporter interviewing for an article on anorexia).

The therapists can also carry out the interview with just one family in role reversal observed by the rest of the group.

Feedback
Group feedback from the task is carried out in the main group. Therapists encourage conversations and curiosity about what they have heard in the task. In particular it is helpful to find points of recognition of similarities and differences.

Parents' comments about this exercise

- Another good one for empathising
- One of the complaints the girls had about the parents was not being listened to. I think it gave the girls quite a surprise to hear actually how much the parents had heard and how well their parents knew and recognised how they were feeling. Even if

MFT activities

the parents could and should not give into girls wanting more trust but actually being at a stage of anorexia where parents could not give it.

Care tags

Aims:

Support participants to explore their own emotional responses and what makes them feel supported

Increase communication within families about how to manage strong emotions in helpful ways

Participants and format: Young people and siblings / Whole group together

Related themes: Managing relationships / Independence / Promoting empathy and understanding

Typical phase of treatment: Follow-up days 1, 2 or 3

Materials:

Pens

Paper

Care tags handout

Craft material

The activity is based around the "washing instructions" that all clothing has – such as "do not iron", "cold wash only", "delicate" etc. The idea is to support young people (or all group members) to think of what their "care tags" would be for themselves and their emotions.

If you decide to do it all together it is important to make it clear that parents do not feed their care tags back to the young people, but that young people will feed back to parents. If parents do create care tags, it is usually only to be shared with partners. This is to ensure that young people do not feel as though they need to "look after" their parents and helps parents to remain in a parenting role.

Instructions for therapists

1. Separate the group as desired. This can either be young people alone or it can be a task for everyone.
2. Provide everyone with pens, paper, craft material, and handouts.
3. Instruct everyone that they will be creating care tags for themselves that outline exactly how they feel most cared for. For example: "If an alien were to come to earth today and they needed to know how to look after you what would they need to know".
4. Provide Care tags handout (see Figure 14.3).

Option: If participants are struggling with such open instructions, facilitators might wish to offer more specific guidelines. You can use the example below (see Figure 14.3), which will guide participants to think about a few specific emotions, and then to think about what they need at those times.

Participants are encouraged to be as playful and creative as possible. They might also wish to decorate their care tags or put string around them etc.

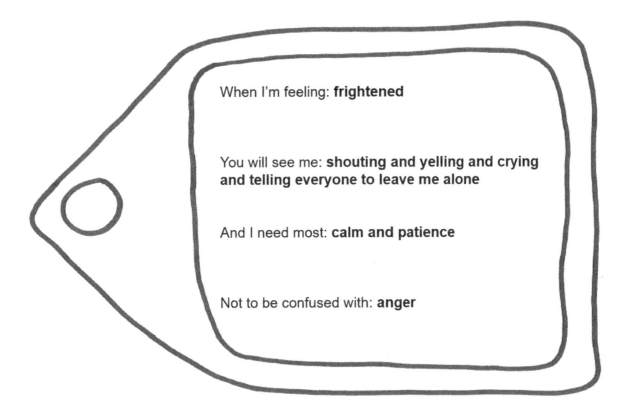

14.3
Care tags

Feedback
In the first part of the feedback, young people (including siblings) form a small huddle with their parents / family to feed back what they have done and show their tags. Then, in the wider group, feedback is invited from parents and young people about both the content of the tags, as well as the process of making them.

Notes
The aim of this task is less about having perfect care tags, but rather for participants to think about and communicate to their families what feels supportive to them.

1, 2, 3 Reveal

Aims:
Help individuals communicate with family members about family relationships in a quick and non-threatening way

Participants and format: Whole group together, separated into pairs or groups of three within families

Related themes: Managing relationships / Independence / Promoting empathy and understanding

Typical phase of treatment: Follow-up days 1, 2 or 3

Materials:
Pens
Paper

MFT activities

1, 2, 3 Reveal helps groups of two to three family members to have important conversations and voice opinions in a new way. This conversation may be about family dynamics (as the example questions suggest), but can equally be adapted to any topic that is important to the group to address.

Instructions for therapists

1. Separate people into pairs or threes within their own family.
2. Provide everyone with pens and paper.
3. Read out questions that participants must quickly write an answer to on the paper without showing their partner.
4. Ask them to reveal their response to their partner/s on the count one, two, three **reveal**.

Example questions and sequence:

Who loses keys most often in your family?
Who is the funniest in your family?
Who is the first to make you laugh?
Who is the first on the dance floor?
Which two people are best at making up after a row?
Who is most likely to hold onto hope in your family?
Who do you feel most protective of?
Who is the peace maker?
Who is most likely to stay calm when things are tricky?
Who is most likely to try something new when things are difficult?
If you were a sinking ship who would take charge?
Who in your family is anorexia most afraid of?
Who in your family is most afraid of anorexia?

Feedback

Allow a brief conversation in pairs / small groups about responses, then get feedback as a whole group once all questions are answered.

Getting feedback in the wider group can ensure that private conversations will be "on record", discussed and processed. Participants are reminded that they can share as much or as little as they are comfortable with.

Family and social circles

Aims:
Strengthen social networks and support
Focus on life beyond the eating disorder
Participants and format: Whole group together
Related themes: Thinking beyond the eating disorder
Typical phase of treatment: Follow-up days 2, 3 or 4
Materials:
Pens
Large pieces of paper

Follow-up days and exercises

Instructions for therapists

1. Explain how important connections, e.g. to close family members, extended family, friends, colleagues, church members, school teachers, hobby groups, online connections etc. all have a role. In often very different ways, our social connections are nurturing us as human beings and helping us to keep a sense of our own identity in different areas of our lives.
2. Instruct the group, either as individuals or as a family to use a large piece of paper on which they draw themselves at the centre, and then begin to plot all those important connections with other people that surround them. They should be instructed to indicate how close or important these various connections are.

Feedback

Families / individuals feedback their "circles" to the whole group.

Notes

The exercise is also helpful in starting the process of expanding the families' and individuals' horizons as they emerge from the illness and enter the final phase of treatment.

Developing a visual map, which serves as a reminder of the extent of the support and nurturance that surrounds the family or individual family members.

Body image T-shirts

Aims:
Open discussion around body image for everyone, not just young people
Promote healthy body image
Understand negative influences and how to manage them

Participants and format: Whole group together, separated into smaller groups (mothers, fathers, young people, siblings)

Related themes: Body image

Typical phase of treatment: Follow-up days 1, 2 or 3

Materials:
Plain T-shirts (or flip-chart paper with T-shirts drawn)
Fabric pens

Instructions for therapists

1. Provide each group with a T-shirt (or make a front and back of a T-shirt from flip chart sheets, which can then be stapled together)
2. Ask the groups to illustrate the front of the T-Shirt with all the messages received about body-image that arise through peer pressure, the media, anorexia (e.g. you must be thin, toned, pretty, blemish-free etc.).
3. Ask them to illustrate on the reverse of the T-shirt all those things that they can appreciate about their bodies, e.g. lungs that can breathe, skin that protects, muscles and bones that help us to move and dance / swim etc.
4. An option is to use different colours to identify different sources of influence (society, media, peers, family, myself).
5. Each group selects one member to wear the T-shirt for a "fashion parade" for the rest of the group to see.

MFT activities

Feedback

Feedback is given to the whole group by the individual groups.

Encourage feedback that focuses not so much on how people feel about their body, rather what influences it, what promotes healthy body image, how it can be shared, and how to have these discussions in helpful ways moving forward. It is important to link everyone's experiences together and not to solely focus on the body image of the young people.

Notes

This exercise is helpful in later phases of the MFT and focuses on body-image as something that not only affects people with anorexia but everyone, including parents, to a greater or lesser extent.

Activities targeting facing uncertainty and exploring independence and autonomy
Social media: friend or foe?

Aims:
   Open up discussion about social media and how it interacts with eating disorder symptoms
   Generate ideas on how to use social media in a positive way

Participants and format: Whole group together, separated into reconstituted / foster families

Related themes: Thinking beyond the eating disorder / Promoting independence / Managing relationships

Typical phase of treatment: Follow-up days 3, 4 or 5

Materials:
   Paper
   Pens
   Separate spaces for each group

Instructions for therapists

1. Divide participants into groups of three or four. Each group should comprise one young person and two adults, preferably each group will have a gender mix. Siblings can be attached to any group as long as they are not with a family member.
2. Give all groups the same two questions (below) to discuss together. Tell each group to record themes or ideas on paper and to choose who will present feedback to the larger group.

Question 1: What is the impact of social media on eating disorders?
   Question 2: In what ways does being competitive online get played out with anorexia?

Feedback

When the large group reconvenes for feedback, ask one young person to scribe on flip-chart paper for the whole group.

It is important to discuss the feedback from the perspective of both the positives and negatives of social media use. This activity can be a useful time to provide psychoeducation about the relationship between social media use and self-esteem.

Follow-up days and exercises

Notes

Discussing social media during treatment is crucial due to its powerful impact on the lives of young people. This task aims to generate discussion particularly with regard to the online competitiveness of young people with anorexia. This exercise offers an opportunity to think about the pros, cons, pitfalls and occasional secretiveness linked to social-media use.

Press conference on anorexia

Aims:
- Enhance parental understanding and knowledge of the *experience* of anorexia
- Allow young people to talk about what anorexia is like in a less direct and threatening way and from a different perspective

Participants and format: Whole group together (with some time spent separately at first)

Related themes: Understanding the experience of having an eating disorder / Increased communication

Typical phase of treatment: Follow-up days 3, 4 or 5

Materials:
- A panel to sit behind something (e.g. a desk)
- Clipboards
- Pens
- Paper
- Anything else to make it feel more like a press conference

The anorexia press conference is a task that allows all participants to take new roles in order to think about the illness in new ways. The task uses the metaphor of a "press conference" to intentionally elevate young people into an expert role and parents into a curious role about the experience of having an eating disorder, rather than what an eating disorder is.

Instructions for therapists

1. Separate the group into parents and young people and take the groups to different rooms.
2. Young people are assigned the role of an expert in a particular field related to anorexia. Examples include experts of family relationships, dietetics, mood difficulties, anxiety, adolescent development etc.
3. Young people are then instructed to brainstorm all of the key things that they would say in relation to each field and to write notes to refer to if necessary. The young people give themselves pseudonyms, e.g. Dr Brilliance, Professor Bright. They sit as a panel of experts on anorexia and their parents are encouraged to ask questions as if they are journalists at a press conference researching anorexia.

MFT activities

4. At the same time, parents are told that they are now journalists and they are about to attend a press conference with experts on anorexia. It will be their job to come up with as many questions as they can to enable them to write a piece on the experience of having anorexia. It is important to emphasise that the article is not about what anorexia is, rather what it is like to experience anorexia. This can be illuminating for parents when young people talk openly about their knowledge of anorexia and offer insights into their thinking about the illness.
5. In order to get into role, they are encouraged to come up with a name for the newspaper they work for and maybe a job title. Parents are also instructed to make the press conference rowdy and to fire questions in a comical manner to try and lighten the mood.
6. The group then comes together, and the press conference is held.

Optional: Following the press conference parents can be assigned an expert on the panel to help them write the short article. Articles are then read back to the wider group.

Feedback

Feedback is carried out in the wider group. The debrief should aim to tread the line between hearing about the silliness of the activity and what this helped people to understand and appreciate in new ways. Young people are invited to comment on whether the articles reflect the real experience or not if this option is taken.

Speed problem-solving

Aims:
Encourage feedback and thinking with people who do not usually interact as much
Promote problem-solving skills
Participants and format: Whole group together
Related themes: Various (dependent on questions)
Typical phase of treatment: Anytime
Materials:
Flip-chart paper
Pens

This exercise has two parts and is helpful at any phase in MFT. It is a useful task when the theme of feeling stuck (families or group) emerges in the morning feedback and group members appear unsure how to move forwards. It is an opportunity to enhance the group capacity to use their skills in problem-solving rather than eliciting the expertise of the therapists.

Instructions for therapists

1. During the first task of the day, ask families to feed back one positive and one challenge since they last met with the group. Make a note on flip-chart paper of this conversation encouraging detail and discussion between families.
2. During the morning break staff reflect on the feedback and identify themes.

Follow-up days and exercises

3. Choose the most relevant three to five themes and turn each theme into a question. See examples below.
4. Write each question on the top of separate pieces of flip-chart paper. One question per page.
5. Organise the room into separate areas, each with a table and chairs around it. Place one question on each table. If you do not have tables, a circle of chairs also works well.
6. Divide the whole group into smaller groups comprising a mixture of young people, parents and siblings, preferably all from different families. The number of questions you have identified needs to match the number of groups created. For example, if five questions are identified, then you will need five groups.
7. Allocate each group to a question, ask them to move to the corresponding area and provide pens. The groups are then asked to generate ideas about answering their allocated question and to write them down on the flip-chart paper. Give 20 minutes to work on the first question. Encourage the groups to consider the order and timing of different solutions. Ideally, give each group pens of a particular colour so that it can easily be determined later which group contributed particular ideas.
8. After 20 minutes tell the groups to physically move on to the next area and question. Instruct them to first look at the work already generated by the previous group and then add to what has been written with their own, new ideas. Give them 10 minutes for this round.
9. Repeat this pattern, giving each group less and less time to find solutions.
10. Each group should have the opportunity to discuss and problem-solve solutions for every question.
11. Groups should finish on the question they started with.

Some example questions can include:

How can you help young people to open up?
How do you manage your own distress or help your child to manage distress when things get hard?
What do parents need to do to get the tone right when supporting meals?
How do you make sure you "go through" the anorexia rather than around it?
What can't I ignore any longer in order to move forward in recovery?
How do you repair relationships after moments of conflict?
How do we move on from weighing everything?
How do we safely start handing back independence?
How will we know when it is time to get rid of the meal plan?

Feedback

It is important to invite feedback in the wider circle to ensure new ideas are explored and processed. Feedback can be initiated in whatever way is helpful, with the therapists encouraging the group to discuss together the ideas that have been generated by them all. Typically, this would involve each group standing up and providing feedback on the responses generated to the question they have finished on. Discussion points might focus on new or surprising ideas that were generated, or on which of all the ideas are most helpful and why.

MFT activities

Tolerating uncertainty

Aims:
    Encourage families and individuals to think about what might get in the way of moving towards a position of tolerating uncertainty (Phase 3)
    Understanding the role of anxiety in recovery and introducing the concept of "safe uncertainty"

Participants and format: Whole group together

Related themes: Managing independence / Looking forward and coping ahead / Managing anxiety

Typical phase of treatment: Early during follow-up (usually days 2 or 3)

Materials:
    Large enough space
    Flip-chart paper
    Pens
    Tape

Tolerating uncertainty conversations help facilitate thinking about feelings of stuckness, and how to move forward as individuals and as a family. It offers a way of discussing and validating anxiety, and its role in maintaining these feelings of stuckness or fears about taking safe risks that would help them move to the next phase of treatment and start experimenting with flexibility.

During this task participants are introduced to the idea of "safe uncertainty" as a position that is important for everyone to work towards in order to promote change and new learning. While participants often say they would like safety and certainty in most areas of their life, the idea that this will inhibit development and growth is introduced. If everything was certain and safe all the time, there is no room for fun, excitement, new learning, failure or change. This is true of all aspects of life, including recovery from an eating disorder. This task supports individuals to consider where they are currently positioned around recovery, as well as other areas of their life, and where they need to be in order to continue to progress.

Instructions for therapists

1. Draw the graph above on flip-chart paper so that the whole group can see, giving a brief explanation of the concepts.
2. Divide the room into four quadrants using tape or rope to mark the floor according to Figure 14.4.
3. Read out different scenarios and ask participants to physically position themselves in the room based on their answer (start with general situations, before moving to illness-related situations or illness change questions).
4. While participants are in position, facilitators "interview" different people on where they have placed themselves and why (or ask participants in the same quadrant to ask each other about their position). If people are confused, facilitators can demonstrate by placing themselves in the room as an example.

	Safe	
Safe Certainty	Safe Uncertainty
Certain		**Uncertain**
Unsafe Certainty	Unsafe Uncertainty
	Unsafe	

14.4
Safe uncertainty
Adapted from: Mason, 1993

General scenarios

- Sitting an exam
- Attending a job interview
- First day of new school
- Deleting a social media account
- Going on an unplanned holiday with no itinerary
- Telling a friend who has done something wrong that they have upset you

Illness scenarios

- Early on in the illness
- At the beginning of treatment
- Where you are now
- Where you would like to be

Illness change questions

- Ask everyone to stand in the Unsafe Uncertainty (UU) quadrant and think of a time when they would have been there and what made it feel Uncertain and Unsafe
- Ask everyone to think back to what they and other family members did in order for them to move out of that position – once they have that in their mind they can move to the appropriate quadrant.

Variants

- Which quadrant do you like to be in most?
- Which quadrant does anorexia like the most?

MFT activities

- In which quadrant do we have the most fun?
- In which quadrant do we learn the most?
- Which quadrant does your mother /father /daughter / son / sibling like the most?

Feedback

It is important that therapists emphasise that while certainty and safety help us to reduce anxiety, if this is sustained, we cannot grow, develop or recover. This is true of all participants – parents, siblings and young people. The conversation can then turn to "what level of safe uncertainty" is helpful and how much can people manage now. It is important for facilitators to be aware that talking about flexibility too early in the process of MFT might feel threatening and increase anxiety. Similarly, different people within families might have different levels of desired "safe uncertainty", which can lead to arguments or to people feeling criticised – something to be mindful of when debriefing this activity. A helpful theme that can also be developed is to describe the FT-AN model of therapy as progressing from UU / Unsafe Certainty (UC) through Safe Certainty (SC) to Safe Uncertainty (SU).

Everything you've always wanted to know but have been too afraid to ask

Aims:
Allow new information to be discussed in novel ways
Shift roles to promote new thinking

Participants and format: Whole group together

Related themes: Promoting understanding / Managing independence / Managing adolescent issues

Typical phase of treatment: Midway through follow-up / Later on during follow-up

Materials:
Enough space or rooms to split the group into "expert panels"

This exercise allows young people to ask questions they may have been afraid to ask adults or their parents while the adults can offer helpful advice and pass on their knowledge of the world.

Instructions for therapists
Option 1

1. Instruct parents to adopt the role of experts in adolescence and to form an "expert" panel.
2. The young people are supported to develop a list of questions to put to the "experts".
3. Tell the young people that this is an opportunity to ask questions they have always wanted to ask their parents but were too afraid to do so. Tell them that questions might be more general for example parental personal experiences during adolescence and young adulthood rather than about eating disorders.
4. Place "expert" parents seated as a panel with the young people as an audience (resembling Question Time).

Option 2

1. Parents are mixed up and divided into smaller panels. Each parent panel has their own space.
2. The young people spend ten minutes with each panel asking the "expert" panel two questions they identified as relevant to them.
3. After ten minutes they move to the next panel and pose the same two questions.
4. The group therapists co-ordinate the timing as the adolescents rotate from one parental "expert" panel to the next. Each panel is instructed that they need to answer questions posed and can't use the "fifth amendment".

Feedback

The feedback of this activity is usually less focused on what people's questions were, but more about what they learnt. The role-shifting is also a useful topic to reflect on. One common theme to elicit, is the idea that parents know more than perhaps young people expect and that they might be more of a resource than previously believed.

What's old is new and what's new is old

Aims:
- Help parents reconnect with their own youth, including the challenges and the strengths / resources they used to overcome them
- Allow young people and siblings to see their parents in a different light and as potential resources

Participants and format: Whole group together

Related themes: Promoting understanding / Managing independence / Managing adolescent issues

Typical phase of treatment: Follow-up days 3, 4 or 5

Materials:
Room with a one-way screen

Instructions for therapists

1. Explain the set-up of the activity and the use of the one-way screen.
2. Place parents in therapy room with young people watching through the one-way screen in the observation room.
3. Ask parents to close their eyes and to cast their mind back in time and to visualise how they looked when they were the same age as their young person.
4. Once they have visualised their appearance (labour the point of mentioning clothing, hair, appearance etc.) move to visualising their bedroom (labour on the details to encourage richness of memory).
5. Then invite parents to open their eyes and start a group discussion about all aspects of their adolescent life including their relationships with friends and families, who they went to for support, what was happening at school, did they have a crush on someone, what were they worried about, the response they received from their peers and parents etc.

MFT activities

6. Once themes have emerged swap young people and parents and while parents are watching, guide a discussion with the young people and siblings about what they have heard and what it changes for them.

Feedback

As with the task above "Everything you've always wanted to know but have been too afraid to ask", the feedback of this task is often centred around what surprised the young people and to generate a conversation with them about how their parents might know more about adolescents and the struggles they face than previously thought. It is useful to connect parents' experiences and strengths to their capacity to be helpful and supportive to their children in the present.

Activities exploring the journey through the illness and linking this with the family lifecycle (past, present and future)
Family journey

Aims:
Putting illness into perspective of family life as a whole
Understanding changes that have occurred and planning for the future
Understanding strengths and anticipating potential future difficulties
Participants and format: Whole group together, families working within their family
Related themes: Addressing adolescent and family lifecycle issues / Planning ahead
Typical phase of treatment: Follow-up days 4, 5 or 6
Materials:
Large pieces of paper
Coloured pens / pencils

The task offers an opportunity for families to reminisce or for family members to be curious about past events. It encourages dialogue and curiosity about who they are and where they have come from. It offers an opportunity for families to reflect on their history, celebrate their achievements and talk about the adversities they have endured.

Instructions for therapists

1. Give each family a large piece of paper and ask them to illustrate on the paper their family's life journey. They can illustrate this in whatever way makes sense to them; they can draw this as a map of roads, towns, villages, mountains etc. or as a river from its source to the sea with tributaries, lakes and meanders. They can choose where their story will begin; from parents meeting or from the birth of their first child.
2. Encourage them to talk together as they map out their life's journey; which stories have been forgotten and only now remembered and which are "family favourites"? Where was the terrain hard going and where were the waters calm?

Feedback

The focus of the feedback is often on how the family manages difficulties and how they celebrate achievements and strengths. The task offers an opportunity for connection as a way of strengthening relationships as they move into the future. Again, this activity offers an opportunity for all group members to talk about what they have learnt as a result of the eating disorder entering the family and what things they would like to hold onto as they move into the future.

Trip down memory lane

Aims:

Support individuals and families to remember or re-remember old things about themselves or the family that may have been sidelined or lost while anorexia was present

Encourage individuals and families to remember old strengths.

Participants and format: Whole group together

Related themes: Identifying and remembering individual and family strengths / Planning ahead / Relapse prevention

Typical phase of treatment: Follow-up days 4, 5 or 6

Materials:

Participants need to bring in an object or photo from home that represents something about them as a family

This activity encourages a reconnection with the past and a focus on important memories, which may have been buried under the weight of coping with the illness. This exercise requires advanced planning as it involves individuals bringing in photographs or other items from home that have special meaning to them. It is usually introduced at the third or fourth follow-up in order to be carried out at the next follow-up.

Instructions for therapists

1. Write a letter to, or ask group members in advance (previous follow-up) to bring in at least one, but preferably up to three photos or important, transportable items, which represent important memories or connections to the past. Advise everyone not to talk in their families about which items they will bring and advise that they should bring items or images which they are prepared to talk about in the group. Often families will ask if they have to bring photos "before and after anorexia" in which case they should be told that it is up to them.
2. The task can be carried out in different ways; the group can be split up into random groupings of mixed adults and young people, they can be split into mothers, fathers and young people, or the exercise can be done with all family members together.
3. Whichever way you choose, explain that each person should have around five to ten minutes to talk about their items / photos and that people should be curious and ask questions about what they hear and see.

Feedback

Feedback to the group is focused not only on what group members found interesting but also on the process itself, emphasising the way in which anorexia will often rob people and families of the capacity or energy to think back and forwards in time as the illness arrests them in the present.

Individuals and the group as a whole are encouraged to be reflective and curious, to ask about memories prompted by the photos or memorabilia and talk with one another about their respective experiences and memories.

MFT activities

"Back to the future" tea party

Aims:
Increase motivation for remaining well
Promote reflection and preparation for life post-anorexia
Participants and format: Whole group together, young people in fishbowl
Related themes: Addressing adolescent and family lifecycle issues / Planning ahead / Relapse prevention
Typical phase of treatment: Follow-up days 5 or 6
Materials:
Prop cups and plates
Table and chairs

This is a task carried out in "fishbowl" style by the young people with parents observing in an outer circle. If there are observation facilities (one-way screen, video link) this can enhance the experience. It is an opportunity to imagine a future when treatment is over, when young people are old and reflecting on their journey through childhood, through treatment for anorexia and through adulthood. This task can generate motivation and hope as young people imagine their future lives and parents witness their child's ambitions for the future. It can also allow reflection and preparation for the family's life post anorexia.

Instructions for therapists

1. Bring the young people to the "fishbowl" and tell them to imagine that they have unexpectedly bumped into each other in 50 years' time when they are in their 60s or 70s. They have decided to have tea and chat for a while. They are encouraged to talk about their time as patients in the clinic and to explain to each other how they came to be where they are today. The group may be encouraged to talk about how they came to be here "without" anorexia, or the therapist might choose to leave this part of the conversation to the young people to introduce.
2. The therapist will judge their level of involvement and interjections depending on how the conversation unfolds. Some groups might need more prompting than others and silent members might need encouragement by the therapist to join in with questions about their life as an adult.
3. Parents listen and are then encouraged to talk about the experience. Young people are also encouraged to talk about what the process was like for them.

Feedback

It is important to ensure that the debrief of this task is for young people and "observers" alike. While the content is important to think about, again asking questions about what it was like to do the task is often very fruitful. If young people struggle to think about the future, this can be important to discuss as it might be an indicator that life is not "getting bigger".

Notes

This activity needs good preparation with young people. It is important to ensure that they have grasped that the intention of the exercise is to reflect on their illness and its impact from the perspective of a future standpoint.

Activities to end MFT
Recovery recipes

> **Aims**:
>   Reflect on the whole recovery process from start to finish in a humorous, non-threatening manner
>
> **Participants and format**: Whole group together, separated into smaller groups (mothers, fathers, young people, siblings) or foster families
>
> **Related themes**: Identifying and remembering individual and family strengths / Planning ahead / Relapse prevention
>
> **Typical phase of treatment**: Final day of follow-up / Very end of treatment
>
> **Materials**:
>   Large pieces of paper
>   Pens

Recovery recipes is a light-hearted way for everyone in the group to reflect on the process of recovery from anorexia from start to end. It encourages people to use the format of a "recipe", to think about the appropriate "ingredients", their amounts and how they are put together to "bake" recovery (see Figure 14.5 for example).

Instructions for therapists

1. Separate participants into smaller groups – either foster families or groups of parents, siblings and young people.
2. Instruct the group that they will need to create a recipe for recovery from anorexia.
3. The recipe should include an ingredients list (with quantities) as well as a method section that will describe the sequence and manner in which the ingredients are put together.
4. Each group feeds back their recipe to the wider group.

Feedback

The feedback for this activity is often very light-hearted, even though it is based around a potentially challenging topic. Discussion around the timing and the quantity of different aspects of recovery are often useful and help families own the process together. The activity can often promote hope as it helps families better understand their strengths as well as acknowledge how far they have come.

The tables are turned

> **Aims**:
>   Demote facilitators from leading the last activity of the group and becoming participants instead
>   Hand over the group process to the participants to manage themselves and for facilitators to step back
>   Reduce dependency on the treating team as equals to mark the ending of the group
>
> **Participants and format**: Whole group together (structure determined by group members, not facilitators)
>
> **Related themes**: Looking towards the future / Having fun

MFT activities

14.5
Recovery
recipe

Typical phase of treatment: Final day of follow-up / Very end of treatment
Materials:
  Whatever the group needs

This task is done at the very end of MFT as a way of the facilitators joining with the group as participants in the process. It allows the group to take charge of the group, to then manage it without facilitation from that point onwards.

Follow-up days and exercises

Instructions for therapists

1. At the end of the second final follow-up day, let all participants know that they will have to prepare an activity for the final follow-up day. The aim of the activity will be for them to decide together how they want to mark the group ending.
2. It is up to the group to discuss and decide what they want the activity to be about, how to run it and what materials will be needed
3. Instruct them to let you know before the final day what materials will be needed or to bring whatever is needed themselves.
4. Emphasise that facilitators will be participants in the task.
5. Offer guidance and assistance as needed. Guidance should be around the practicalities of the task, rather than what the task should be about. The theme of the task is usually around endings and saying goodbye.

Feedback

The point of this activity is partly to have fun. So, enjoy not knowing what will happen and make a point of joining in the uncertainty with the group.

Final "post-it" note task

Aims:
Help everyone to identify strengths and notice resilience in each other
Say goodbye
Participants and format: Whole group together
Related themes: Looking towards the future / Building solidarity / Saying goodbye
Typical phase of treatment: Final day of follow-up / Very end of treatment
Materials:
Post-it notes (enough for one pad per person)
Pens

The final post-it note task provides an opportunity for everyone in the group to support each other individually by offering a comment, strength, memory etc. It is a very personal task and allows people to say goodbye to each other and to punctuate the ending of the group process.

Instructions for therapists

1. Ask each member of the group to write a comment on a post-it note related to each member of the group.
2. Ask them to write down each person's best quality and what they wish for them for their future. Once all group members have had time to complete their post-it notes for all members of the group, ask them to stick their post-it notes relating to each person on the wall around each group member's name.
3. At the end of the task invite each member to collect the post-it notes around their name and take them home with them.

Feedback

None required; however, some people might want to say thank you or highlight a comment that felt particularly nice.

MFT activities

The final reflection

Aims:
Allow the group to reflect on the journey of MFT all together

Participants and format: Whole group together

Related themes: Looking towards the future / Building solidarity / Saying goodbye

Typical phase of treatment: Final day of follow-up / Very end of treatment

Materials: None

This task is simply to offer the group a space to think about the MFT journey as a group.

Instructions for therapists

1. Offer a short amount of time (20 min.) to reflect together on the MFT journey.
2. You may want to leave the discussion very unguided. Alternatively, also guide the group.
3. Typically, this would involve starting with a reflection on how things were for individuals and families at the beginning of MFT, followed by moving forward in time by thinking about the journey itself, including highs, lows and significant turning points.
4. Finally bring the group to reflect on where they are now and what is ahead.

Feedback
None

References

Ackerman, N.W. (1945). What constitutes intensive psychotherapy in a child guidance clinic. *The American Journal of Orthopsychiatry, 15*(4), 711–720 https://doi.org/10.1111/j.1939-0025.1945.tb06543.x.

Apter, N. (2003). The human being: JL Moreno's vision in psychodrama. *International Journal of Psychotherapy, 8*(1), 31–36.

Areemit, R.S., Katzman, D.K., Pinhas, L. & Kaufman, M.E. (2010). The experience of siblings of adolescents with eating disorders. *Journal of Adolescent Health, 46*(6), 569–576. https://doi.org/10.1016/j.jadohealth.2009.12.011.

Asen, E., Dawson, N. & McHugh, B. (2001). *Multiple Family Therapy: The Marlborough Model and its Wider Applications*. Karnac Books.

Asen, E. & Scholz, M. (2010). *Multi-family therapy: Concepts and Techniques*. Routledge.

Bion, W.R. (1962). *Learning from Experience*. Heinemann.

Blessitt, E., Baudinet, J., Simic, M. & Eisler, I. (2020). Eating disorders in children, adolescents and young adults. In K.S. Wampler (Ed.), *The Handbook of Systemic Family Therapy* (pp. 397–425). Wiley & Sons.

Bowlby, J. (1988). *A Secure Base: Parent-Child Attachment and Healthy Human Development*. Routledge.

Butler, G. (1998). Clinical formulation. In A.S. Bellack & M. Hersen (Eds.), *Comprehensive Clinical Psychology* (pp. 1–23). Pergamon.

Cardi, V., Matteo, R.D., Corfield, F. & Treasure, J. (2013). Social reward and rejection sensitivity in eating disorders: an investigation of attentional bias and early experiences. *The World Journal of Biological Psychiatry, 14*(8), 622–633. https://doi.org/10.3109/15622975.2012.665479.

Carrot, B., Duclos, J., Barry, C., Radon, L., Maria, A.S., Kaganski, I., ... & Gerardin, P. (2019). Multicenter randomized controlled trial on the comparison of multi-family therapy (MFT) and systemic single-family therapy (SFT) in young patients with anorexia nervosa: study protocol of the THERAFAMBEST study. *Trials, 20*(1), 1–14. https://doi.org/10.1186/s13063-019-3347-y.

Cassin, S.E. & von Ranson, K.M. (2005). Personality and eating disorders: a decade in review. *Clinical Psychology Review, 25*(7), 895–916. https://doi.org/10.1016/j.cpr.2005.04.012.

Cook-Darzens, S., Gelin, Z. & Hendrick, S. (2018). Evidence base for Multiple Family Therapy (MFT) in non-psychiatric conditions and problems: a review (part 2). *Journal of Family Therapy, 40*(3), 326–343. https://doi.org/10.1111/1467-6427.12177C.

References

Couturier, J., Isserlin, L., Norris, M., Spettigue, W., Brouwers, M., Kimber, M., ... & Snelgrove, N. (2020). Canadian practice guidelines for the treatment of children and adolescents with eating disorders. *Journal of Eating Disorders*, *8*(1), 4. https://doi.org/10.1186/s40337-020-0277-8.

Dare, C. & Eisler, I. (2000). A multi-family group day treatment programme for adolescent eating disorder. *European Eating Disorders Review*, *8*(1), 4–18. https://doi.org/10.1002/(SICI)1099-0968(200002)8:1<4::AID-ERV330>3.0.CO;2-P.

Dawson, L., Baudinet, J., Tay, E. & Wallis, A. (2018). Creating community – the introduction of multi-family therapy for eating disorders in Australia. *Australian and New Zealand Journal of Family Therapy*, *39*(3), 283–293. https://doi.org/10.1002/anzf.1324.

Dennhag, I., Henje, E. & Nilsson, K. (2019). Parental caregiver burden and recovery of adolescent anorexia nervosa after multi-family therapy. *Eating Disorders,* 1–17. https://doi.org/10.1080/10640266.2019.1678980.

Dimitropoulos, G., Klopfer, K., Lazar, L. & Schacter, R. (2009). Caring for a sibling with anorexia nervosa: a qualitative study. *European Eating Disorders Review*, *17*(5), 350–365. https://doi.org/10.1002/erv.937.

Eisler, I. (2005). The empirical and theoretical base of family therapy and multiple family day therapy for adolescent anorexia nervosa. *Journal of Family Therapy*, *27*(2), 104–131. https://doi.org/10.1111/j.1467-6427.2005.00303.x.

Eisler, I. & Lask, J. (2008). Family interviewing and family therapy. In M. Rutter, D. Bishop, D. Pine, S. Scott, J. Stevenson, E. Taylor & A. Thapar (Eds.), *Rutter's Child and Adolescent Psychiatry* (pp. 1062–1078). Wiley Blackwell.

Eisler, I., Simic, M., Blessit, E., Dodge, E. & team (2016b) *Maudsley service model for the management of child and adolescent eating disorders*. Unpublished manuscript. Maudsley Centre for Child and Adolescent Eating Disorders, South London & Maudsley NHS Foundation Trust. www.national.slam.nhs.uk/wp-content/uploads/2011/11/Maudsley-Service-Manual-for-Child-and-Adolescent-Eating-Disorders-July-2016.pdf.

Eisler, I., Simic, M., Hodsoll, J., Asen, E., Berelowitz, M., Connan, F., ... & Landau, S. (2016a). A pragmatic randomised multi-centre trial of multifamily and single family therapy for adolescent anorexia nervosa. *BMC Psychiatry*, *16*(1), 422. https://doi.org/10.1186/s12888-016-1129-6.

Eisler, I., Wallis, A. & Dodge, E. (2015). What's new is old and what's old is new: the origins and evolution of eating disorders family therapy. In K.L. Loeb, D. Le Grange & J. Lock (Eds.), *Family Therapy for Adolescent Eating and Weight Disorders: New Applications* (pp. 26–62). Routledge.

Ellison, R., Rhodes, P., Madden, S., Miskovic, J., Wallis, A., Baillie, A., ... & Touyz, S. (2012). Do the components of manualized family-based treatment for anorexia nervosa predict weight gain? *International Journal of Eating Disorders*, *45*(4), 609–614. https://doi.org/10.1002/eat.22000.

Fonagy, P. (2006). The mentalization-focused approach to social development. In J.G. Allen & P. Fonagy (Eds.), *The Handbook of Mentalization-Based Treatment*, (pp. 53–99). John Wiley & Sons Inc.

Foulkes, S.H. (1948) *Introduction to Group-Analytic Psychotherapy*. Reprinted 1983, Karnac Books.

Frank, G.K., DeGuzman, M.C. & Shott, M.E. (2019). Motivation to eat and not to eat – the psycho-biological conflict in anorexia nervosa. *Physiology & Behavior*, *206*, 185–190. https://doi.org/10.1016/j.physbeh.2019.04.007.

References

Frank, G.K. (2019). Neuroimaging and eating disorders. *Current Opinion in Psychiatry*, *32*(6), 478–483. https://doi.org/10.1097/YCO.0000000000000544.

Frank, G.K., Roblek, T., Shott, M.E., Jappe, L.M., Rollin, M.D., Hagman, J.O. & Pryor, T. (2012). Heightened fear of uncertainty in anorexia and bulimia nervosa. *International Journal of Eating Disorders*, *45*(2), 227–232. https://doi.org/10.1002/eat.20929.

Gabel, K., Pinhas, L., Eisler, I., Katzman, D. & Heinmaa, M. (2014). The effect of multiple family therapy on weight gain in adolescents with anorexia nervosa: pilot data. *Journal of the Canadian Academy of Child and Adolescent Psychiatry*, *23*(3), 196–199.

Gelin, Z., Cook-Darzens, S. & Hendrick, S. (2018). The evidence base for multiple family therapy in psychiatric disorders: a review (part 1). *Journal of Family Therapy*, *40*(3), 302–325. https://doi.org/10.1111/1467-6427.12178.

Gelin, Z., Fuso, S., Hendrick, S., Cook-Darzens, S. & Simon, Y. (2015). The effects of a multiple family therapy on adolescents with eating disorders: an outcome study. *Family Process*, *54*(1), 160–172. https://doi.org/10.1111/famp.12103.

Grienenberger, J.F. (2007). Group process as a holding environment facilitating the development of the parental reflective function. *Psychoanalytic Inquiry*, *26*(4), 668–675. https://doi.org/10.1080/07351690701310714.

Halmi, K.A., Sunday, S.R., Strober, M., Kaplan, A., Woodside, D.B., Fichter, M., ... & Kaye, W. H. (2000). Perfectionism in anorexia nervosa: variation by clinical subtype, obsessionality, and pathological eating behavior. *American Journal of Psychiatry*, *157*(11), 1799–1805. https://doi.org/10.1176/appi.ajp.157.11.1799.

Hambrook, D., Oldershaw, A., Rimes, K., Schmidt, U., Tchanturia, K., Treasure, J., ... & Chalder, T. (2011). Emotional expression, self-silencing, and distress tolerance in anorexia nervosa and chronic fatigue syndrome. *British Journal of Clinical Psychology*, *50*(3), 310–325.

Hay, P., Chinn, D., Forbes, D., Madden, S., Newton, R., Sugenor, L., ... & Ward, W. (2014). Royal Australian and New Zealand College of Psychiatrists clinical practice guidelines for the treatment of eating disorders. *Australian & New Zealand Journal of Psychiatry*, *48*(11), 977–1008. https://doi.org/10.1177/0004867414555814.

Hill, L., Dagg, D., Levine, M.P., Smolak, L., Johnson, S., Stotz, S.A. & Little, N. (2012). *Family Eating Disorders Manual: Guiding Families Through the Maze of Eating Disorders*. Worthington, OH: Center for Balanced Living.

Hollesen, A., Clausen, L. & Rokkedal, K. (2013). Multiple family therapy for adolescents with anorexia nervosa: a pilot study of eating disorder symptoms and interpersonal functioning. *Journal of Family Therapy*, *35*, 5367. https://doi.org/10.1111/1467-6427.12000.

Jewell, T., Blessitt, E., Stewart, C., Simic, M. & Eisler, I. (2016). Family therapy for child and adolescent eating disorders: a critical review. *Family Process*, *55*(3), 577–594. https://doi.org/10.1111/famp.12242.

Kaye, W.H., Wierenga, C.E., Bailer, U.F., Simmons, A.N., & Bischoff-Grethe, A. (2013). Nothing tastes as good as skinny feels: the neurobiology of anorexia nervosa. *Trends in Neurosciences*, *36*(2), 110–120. https://doi.org/10.1016/j.tins.2013.01.003.

Lang, K., Larsson, E.E., Mavromara, L., Simic, M., Treasure, J. & Tchanturia, K. (2016). Diminished facial emotion expression and associated clinical characteristics in Anorexia Nervosa. *Psychiatry Research*, *236*, 165–172. https://doi.org/10.1016/j.psychres.2015.12.004.

Laquer, H.P., La Burt, H.A. & Morong, E. (1964). Multiple family therapy: further developments. *Current Psychiatric Therapies*, *4*, 150–154.

References

Long, M., Verbeke, W., Ein-Dor, T. & Vrtička, P. (2020). A functional neuro-anatomical model of human attachment (NAMA): insights from first- and second-person social neuroscience. *Cortex*, 126, 281–321. doi:10.1016/j.cortex.2020.01.010.

Lopez, C., Tchanturia, K., Stahl, D., Booth, R., Holliday, J. & Treasure, J. (2008). An examination of the concept of central coherence in women with anorexia nervosa. *International Journal of Eating Disorders*, 41(2), 143–152. https://doi.org/10.1002/eat.20478.

Marzola, E., Knatz, S., Murray, S.B., Rockwell, R., Boutelle, K., Eisler, I. & Kaye, W.H. (2015). Short-term intensive family therapy for adolescent eating disorders: 30-month outcome. *European Eating Disorders Review*, 23(3), 210–218. https://doi.org/10.1002/erv.2353.

Mason, B. (1993). Towards positions of safe uncertainty. *Human Systems*, 4, 189–200.

Mehl, A., Tomanová, J., Kuběna, A. & Papežová, H. (2013). Adapting multi-family therapy to families who care for a loved one with an eating disorder in the Czech Republic combined with a follow-up pilot study of efficacy. *Journal of Family Therapy*, 35, 82–101. https://doi.org/10.1111/j.1467-6427.2011.00579.x.

National Institute for Health and Care Excellence. (2017). *Eating Disorders: Recognition and Treatment*. NICE.

Russell, G.F., Szmukler, G.I., Dare, C. & Eisler, I. (1987). An evaluation of family therapy in anorexia nervosa and bulimia nervosa. *Archives of General Psychiatry*, 44(12), 1047–1056. https:/doi.org/10.1001/archpsyc.1987.01800240021004.

Salaminiou, E., Campbell, M., Simic, M., Kuipers, E. & Eisler, I. (2017). Intensive multi-family therapy for adolescent anorexia nervosa: an open study of 30 families. *Journal of Family Therapy*, 39(4), 498–513. https://doi.org/10.1111/1467-6427.12075.

Scholz, M. & Asen, E. (2001). Multiple family therapy with eating disordered adolescents: concepts and preliminary results. *European Eating Disorders Review*, 9(1), 33–42. https://doi.org/10.1002/erv.364.

Simic, M. & Eisler, I. (2015). Multi-family therapy. In K.L. Loeb, D. Le Grange & J. Lock (Eds.), *Family Therapy for Adolescent Eating and Weight Disorders: New Applications* (pp. 110–138). Routledge.

Simic, M. & Eisler, I. (2018). Maudsley family therapy for eating disorders. In J. Lebow, A. Chambers & D.C. Breunlin (Eds.), *Encyclopedia of Couple and Family Therapy* (pp. 1–9). Springer.

Solmi, M., Collantoni, E., Meneguzzo, P., Tenconi, E. & Favaro, A. (2019). Network analysis of specific psychopathology and psychiatric symptoms in patients with anorexia nervosa. *European Eating Disorders Review*, 27(1), 24–33. https://doi.org/10.1002/erv.2633.

Stewart, C.S., Baudinet, J., Hall, R., Fiskå, M., Pretorius, N., Voulgari, S., Hunt, K., Eisler, I & Simic, M. (2019). Multi-family therapy for bulimia nervosa in adolescence: a pilot study in a community eating disorder service. *Eating Disorders: Journal of Treatment and Prevention*, 14, 1–17. https://doi.org/10.1080/10640266.2019.1656461.

Tantillo, M., McGraw, J.L.S. & Le Grange, D. (2020). *Multifamily Therapy Group for Young Adults with Anorexia Nervosa: Reconnecting for Recovery*. Routledge.

Voriadaki, T., Simic, M., Espie, J. & Eisler, I. (2015). Intensive multi-family therapy for adolescent anorexia nervosa: adolescents' and parents' day-to-day experiences. *Journal of Family Therapy*, 37(1), 5–23. https://doi.org/10.1111/1467-6427.12067.

Winnicott, D. (1953). Transitional objects and transitional phenomena. *International Journal of Psychoanalysis*, 34, 89–97.

References

Winnicott, D. (1960). The theory of the parent-child relationship. *International Journal of Psychoanalysis, 41*, 585–595.

Wierenga, C.E., Hill, L., Knatz Peck, S., McCray, J., Greathouse, L., Peterson, D., Scott, A., Eisler, I. & Kaye, W.H. (2018). The acceptability, feasibility, and possible benefits of a neurobiologically-informed 5-day multifamily treatment for adults with anorexia nervosa. *International Journal of Eating Disorders*, *51*(8), 863–869. https://doi.org/10.1002/eat.22876.

Yalom, I. D., & Leszcz, M. (1995). The therapeutic factors. *The Theory and Practice of Group Psychotherapy* (pp. 70–101). Basic Books.

**Appendix I
List of activities by theme**

Appendix I: List of activities by theme

Activity name	Typical Theme	Format	Typical stage of treatment
Icebreakers / Introduction / Opening activities			
Hopes and expectations	Engagement	Whole group together	Day 1 / Beginning of treatment
Photo cards	Engagement	Whole group together	Day 1 / Beginning of treatment
Activities for increasing motivation and insight into the illness			
Portraits of anorexia	Engagement / Increased motivation / Increased understanding	Young people only (including siblings if present)	Day 1 / Early in treatment
Pros and cons of anorexia	Engagement / Increased motivation / Increased understanding	Young people and siblings	Day 1 / Early in treatment
Letters from the future	Managing emotions into the future / Endings	Young people only	Anytime
Writing with non-dominant hand	Engagement / Insight into illness / Motivation	Foster families (young person + parents from other families)	Early in treatment
Activities exploring symptom management and mealtimes			
Preparation for first MFT lunch	Managing eating disorder symptoms / Mealtimes	Parents only	Day 1 / Beginning of treatment
Sunday lunch	Managing eating disorder symptoms / Mealtimes	Working within family groups or individually	Day 2 / Beginning of treatment
Mealtime role reversal	Managing eating disorder symptoms / Mealtimes	Whole group together	Day 2 / Beginning of treatment
Foster family lunch	Managing eating disorder symptoms / Mealtimes	Foster families (as decided by MFT team)	Day 2
Activities exploring the impact of the illness on relationships over time			
Family sculpt	Impact of illness / Managing relationships	Whole group together	Day 3
Family crest	Family strengths / Managing relationships	Working within family groups	Day 3 / Early in treatment
Sibling group	Family and individual coping / Recognition of similarities in experience	Siblings (grouped by age), with 1–2 experienced therapists depending on size and variation of ages of group	Day 3

Appendix I: List of activities by theme

Activity name	Typical Theme	Format	Typical stage of treatment
Validation parent exercise	Managing emotions / Improving relationships	Parents only	Day 2 / Day 3 / Day 4 / Early during follow-up
Traps and treasures	Promoting trust / Listening together / Working together / Having fun	Whole group together	Day 3 / Day 4 / Early in treatment
Where do we stand?	Managing relationships	Parents only / Whole group together	Day 4 / Early during follow-up
Activities exploring looking forward and coping ahead			
Family timelines	Looking forward / Coping ahead	Working within family groups	Day 4
Toolboxes	Managing emotions into the future	Separated groups (mothers, fathers, young people, siblings)	Day 4 (final task)
Closing activities for the four-day intensive workshop			
Photo cards	Managing emotions into the future / Endings	Whole group together	Day 4 (final task)
Pebble and balloon	Managing emotions into the future / Endings	Whole group together	Day 4 (final task)
Letter to future self	Looking forward / Fostering self-reflection	Working individually	Day 4 (final task)
Note to self	Looking forward to trying out something new	Working individually	Day 4 (final task)
Mindfulness exercises			
Ball pattern exercise	Managing emotions	Whole group together	End of Day 1 / End of Day 2 / End of Day 3
Other mindfulness exercises	Manging emotions and distress, mindfulness to breath, etc	Whole group together	End of Day 1, 2 or 3 and follow up days
Introductory activities for follow-up days			
Letter from the previous day	Fostering insight and learning	Working individually	Follow-up
Headlines	Gathering information / Fostering insight and learning / Reinforcing changes	Separated into parents and children (young people and siblings) / Working within family groups	Follow-up Day 1

Appendix I: List of activities by theme

	Applicable to all themes	Whole group together	Follow-up Day 2–3 onwards
Speed dating			
Spaghetti towers	Working together / Having fun	Working within family groups	Anytime

Activities targeting motivation, challenging behavioural patterns and their exits, and increasing mutual understanding

Brain scan	Increased understanding / Improving communication	Working within family groups / individually	Early during follow-up
Breaking the chain	Managing conflict / Maintaining relationships	Working within family groups	Early during follow-up
Motivation see-saws	Motivation / Looking forward / Managing uncertainty	Small groups / foster families	Follow-up Day 1–3

Activities targeting building relationships, social networks, and reflecting on body image

"Internalised other" interview	Managing relationships / Independence / Promoting empathy and understanding	Whole group together, separated into parents and young people	Early during follow-up
Care tags	Managing relationships / Independence / Promoting empathy and understanding	Young people and siblings only	Early during follow-up
1, 2, 3 Reveal	Managing relationships / Independence / Promoting empathy and understanding	Groups of two's or three's within own family	Early during follow-up
Family and social circles	Managing relationships / Independence / Promoting empathy and understanding	Working within family groups / individually	Early during follow-up
Body image T-shirts	Body image	Small groups (mothers, fathers, young people, siblings)	Later on during follow-up

Activities targeting facing uncertainty and exploring independence and autonomy

Social media: friend or foe?	Thinking beyond the eating disorder / Promoting independence / Managing relationships	Small groups / Foster families	Midway through follow-up
Press conference on anorexia	Understanding the experience of having an eating disorder / Increased communication	Whole group together (with some time spent separately at first)	Early during follow-up / Midway through follow-up
Speed problem-solving	Various (dependent on questions)	Whole group together	Anytime
Tolerating uncertainty	Managing independence / Looking forward and coping ahead / Managing anxiety	Whole group together	Early during follow-up (usually Day 2 or 3)

Appendix I: List of activities by theme

Activity name	Typical Theme	Format	Typical stage of treatment
Everything you've always wanted to know but have been too afraid to ask	Promoting understanding / Managing independence / Managing adolescent issues	Whole group together	Midway through follow-up / Later on during follow-up
What's old is new and what's new is old	Promoting understanding / Managing independence / Managing adolescent issues	Whole group together	Midway through follow-up
Activities exploring the journey through the illness and linking this with the family lifecycle (Past, Present, and Future)			
Family journey	Addressing adolescent and family lifecycle issues / Planning ahead	Working within family groups	Later on during follow-up
"Back to the future" tea party	Addressing adolescent and family lifecycle issues / Planning ahead / Relapse prevention	Whole group together, young people in fishbowl	Later on during follow-up
Trip down memory lane	Identifying and remembering individual and family strengths / Planning ahead / Relapse prevention	Whole group together	Later on during follow-up
Activities to end MFT			
Recovery recipes	Identifying and remembering individual and family strengths / Planning ahead / Relapse prevention	Small groups / Foster families	Final day of follow-up / Very end of treatment
The tables are turned	Looking towards the future / Having fun	Whole group together (structure determined by participants, not facilitators)	Final day of follow-up / Very end of treatment
Final "post-it" note task	Looking towards the future / Building solidarity / Saying goodbye	Whole group together	Final day of follow-up / Very end of treatment
The final reflection	Looking towards the future / Building solidarity / Saying goodbye	Whole group together	Final day of follow-up / Very end of treatment

**Appendix II
List of activities by format**

Appendix II: List of activities by format

	Whole group working together	Young people	Siblings	Parents	Working within families	Foster families / Small groups	Individual work
Hopes and expectations	X						
Photo cards	X						
Portraits of anorexia		X	X				
Pros and cons of anorexia		X	X				
Letters from the future		X					
Writing with non-dominant hand						X	
Preparation for first MFT lunch				X			
Sunday lunch					X		X
Mealtime role reversal	X						
Foster family lunch						X	
Family sculpt	X				X		
Family crest					X		
Sibling group			X				
Validation parent exercise				X			
Making Treasures (for Traps and Treasures)		X	X				
Traps and treasures	X						
Where do we stand?	X			X			
Family timelines					X		
Toolboxes						X	
Pebble and balloon	X						
Note to future self							X
Ball pattern exercise	X						
Note from the previous day							X

Appendix II: List of activities by format

Activity	1	2	3	4	5	6
Headlines		X				
Speed dating	X					
Spaghetti towers			X			
Brain scan			X			X
Breaking the chain			X			
Motivation see-saws				X		
"Internalised other" interview	X	X				
Care tags	X					
1, 2, 3 Reveal			X			
Family and social circles			X			X
Body image T-shirts				X		
Social media: friend or foe?				X		
Press conference on anorexia	X					
Speed problem-solving	X					
Tolerating uncertainty	X					
Everything you've always wanted to know but have been too afraid to ask	X					
What's old is new and what's new is old	X					
Family journey					X	
"Back to the future" tea party	X					
Trip down memory lane	X					
Recovery recipes				X		
The tables are turned	X					
Final "post-it" note task	X					
The final reflection	X					

Index

Note: Page references to figures are in **bold**, while references to tables are in *italics*.

activities: choosing 38; clinician map to facilitating 42; debrief 41; follow-up days *see* follow-up days and relevant activities; four-day workshop *see* four-day intensive workshop, relevant activities; refusal to take part in 65; relying on participation in front of whole group 65–66; themes 74; toolkits *39*; using in MFT-AN 73–74

adolescents and young people: challenges identified by 80, 82–83, 90, 98; MFT-AN for 3; on workshop activities 80, 82, 92, 94, 98, 105, 108

adult anorexia nervosa 3

affect, managing 58; clinical examples 60; flat affect 60–61; high levels 58–60, **59**; low levels 60–62, **62**; pausing 59–60

anorexia nervosa: exploring individual and family life cycle following 16–17; four phases of family therapy *13*; portraits of 78–83

anxiety 15, 16–17, 21, 55, 57; anxiety disorders 3; clinician/therapist 38, 73; of facilitating 37; at mealtimes 16, 24–25, 53, 54, 90, 93; parental 15; potential 26, 79; raised/heightened 15, 25, 53, 132; reducing 15, 23, 24, 100, 101; validating 130

attunement 9–10

ball pattern activity 112
body image T-shirts 125–126
brain: neurobiology of anorexia nervosa 14–17; scanning of 116–118
brain-body changes 14–15
bulimia nervosa, adolescent 3
bullying 14

care tags 122–123, **123**
catharsis 12
change: of behaviour 21–22; broadening of treatment scope 20–21; community-building 21; experimentation 21–22, 43; facilitating 18–22; factors influencing positive change *11*; indicators of 20; mechanisms of 5–6; multiple sources of input 19–20

closing activities, four-day workshop 110–112
co-facilitators and helpers 32, *33*
community-building 21
containment 9–10; container and the contained concept 9, 11
content of MFT-AN 27–28

debrief 41

eating disorder: competition about symptoms 68; eating disorder-focused family therapy 13–17; supporting families to manage 16

effectiveness of MFT-AN 4–5
emotions: and containment 10; overwhelm, feelings of 11; processing of 11; strong 66; *see also* affect, managing

ending of treatment, and future plans/discharge 17

engagement: deepening 67; disengagement 60, 61; factors impacting 69; group 20, 65; increasing 16, 62, 63; individual 45; levels of 21–22, 36, 55, 58, 65; low attendance at meetings 69; managing low levels 60–62; in MFT activities 88; phases of family therapy 13–17; reasons for lack of 60–61; of whole family 15

evidence for MFT-AN 4
experimentation 21–22, 43
externalisation 15–16

families: journey of 134–135; life cycle, linking to illness 134–136; and social circles 124–125; and suitability for MFT-AN 8; *see also* "foster families"

family crest activity 98–99, **100**
family sculpt activity 22, 51, 65, 94–98
family therapy for anorexia nervosa *see* FT-AN (family therapy for anorexia nervosa)

feedback: and follow-up days *see* feedback, follow-up days; format

Index

43; and four-day workshop *see* feedback, four-day workshop; importance of 41

feedback, follow-up days 115, 117, 121; asking questions 133; "back to the future" tea-party 136; body image T-shirts 126; breaking the chain 118, 119; care tags 123; family and social circles 125; independence 126–127; memory lane 135; 1, 2, 3 reveal 124; recovery recipes 137; speed problem-solving 129; uncertainty, tolerating 126–127, 132

feedback, four-day workshop: on activities to increase motivation and insight 79, 81, 85; on closing activities 111, 112; on impact of illness on relationships over time 97, 99; looking forward and coping ahead 108; on non-dominant hand, writing with 86; on opening activities/icebreakers 78; on sibling groups 101; on symptom management and mealtimes 87, 88, 92, 93–94; toolboxes 109; traps and treasures game 103–104; validation parent activity 102

fishbowl technique 49–50, 61, 90, 92, 93, 97, 136

follow-up days and relevant activities 23, 29–31, 113–137; asking questions 132–133; "back to the future" tea-party 136–140; behaviour patterns 116–120; body image, reflecting on 120–123; breaking the chain 118–119; care tags 122–123; exploring the old and new 133–134; family and social circles 124–125; frequency 3; headlines 114; illness journey, exploring 134–135; introductory activities 113–116; letter from previous day 113; looking to the future 137; low attendance at meetings 69; memory lane 135; motivation challenges 116–120; motivation see-saws 119–120; mutual understanding, increasing 116–120; parental comments 121–122; press conference 127–128; recovery recipes 137, **138**; relationship-building 120–123; social media as a friend or foe 126; social networks 120–123; spaghetti towers activity 115–116; speed dating 114–115; structure 30; themes, examples of *31*; uncertainty, tolerating 130–132

formulation 16

"foster families" 50; lunch 55–57, 93–94

four-day intensive workshop, relevant activities 23, 27, 76–112; challenges identified by young people 80, 82–83, 90, 98; closing activities 110–112; content 27–28; exploring impact of illness on relationships over time 94–101; follow-up days 29–31, 113–137; icebreakers 76–78; to increase motivation and insight 78–85; looking forward and coping ahead 107–110; mindfulness 111–112; non-dominant hand, writing with 85–86; opening 76–78; parents' comments 80, 92, 94, 97–98, 105, 108, 109; photo cards 78, 111–112; preparation for first MFT lunch 86–87; sibling group 99–101; structure 26–27, 28; symptom management and mealtimes, exploring 86–94; themes, examples of 27, *28*; timing 27, 28; toolboxes 108–110; traps and treasures game 102–106; validation parent 101–102; Where do we stand? (activity for parents) 105–106; young people's comments 80, 90, 92, 94, 98, 105, 108; *see also* feedback, four-day workshop; instructions for therapists on four-day intensive workshop

FT-AN (family therapy for anorexia nervosa) 4, 5, 13, 25; Maudsley Family Therapy for Anorexia Nervosa 3; principles 28, 55; structure 20

"graduate family" 26

group process 36, 38–46; basic principles 12; being friendly outside the group 68; choice of activities 38–39; clinical examples 61–62; clinical map to facilitating activities 42; closed groups in MFT 3; control 58; developing a new activity 43; effective management and containment 58–63; facilitating activities 40–41; group cohesion 28; humour and playfulness 46; increasing engagement 62, 63; initiating an irrelevant theme or activity 61–62; insufficient 62, 63; management 38–46, 58–63; parents meeting up outside the group 69; position, proximity and focus 44–45; self, use of 45; sibling groups 101; variability in attendance 4; *see also* four-day intensive workshop, relevant activities; MFT (multi-family therapy); MFT-AN (multi-family therapy for anorexia nervosa); workshop activities

group theories influencing MFT 11–13; group coordinator/administrator 33–34; role of group therapist 12

guilt 15

holding environment 10, 11

hopes and expectations activity 76–77

hormonal changes 14

icebreakers 76–78

illness journey, exploring 134–135

independence and autonomy, supporting 16–17, 126

independent eating, helping to re-establish 16–17

inpatient care 8

insight, activities to increase 78–85

instructions for therapists on follow-up days 116–117, 120; asking questions 132–133; "back to the future" tea-party 136; body

Index

image T-shirts 125; breaking the chain 118–119; care tags 122; exploring the old and new 133–134; family and social circles 125; illness journey, exploring 134–135; introductory activities 114, 115, 116; looking to the future 137; memory lane 135; 1, 2, 3 reveal 124; press conference 128–129; recovery recipes 137; speed problem-solving 128–129; uncertainty, tolerating 126, 130–132
instructions for therapists on four-day intensive workshop: closing activities 110, 111, 112; exploring impact of illness on relationships over time 95–97; looking forward and coping ahead 107–108; motivation and insight, increasing 79, 80–81, 84; non-dominant hand, writing with 85–86; notes to future self 110–111; opening activities/icebreakers 76–77, 78; sibling groups 101; symptom management and mealtimes, exploring 86–87, 89, 91; toolboxes 109; traps and treasures game 103–104; validation parent activity 102; Where do we stand? (activity for parents) 105–106
"internalised other" interview 120–121
interviews 47, 120–122
introductory activities, follow-up days 113–116
introductory afternoon 23–26; "pleading the fifth amendment" metaphor 24, 25
isolation, reducing 21

knowledge: integrating 13; sharing of 12, 19

lead facilitators 32–33, 41, 60
lessons from the future activity 83–85

maladaptive perfectionism 14
Marlborough Family Day Unit, London 3
Maudsley Family Therapy for Anorexia Nervosa 3; *see also* FT-AN (family therapy for anorexia nervosa)
MDT (multidisciplinary team) 13
mealtimes: anxiety at 16, 24, 53, 54, 90, 93; clinician map 55, **56**; dining room separate from main MFT group 54; expectations around 54; first MFT lunch 87–88; foster family lunch 55–57, 93–94; four-day workshop activities 86–94; not eating or finishing a meal 67; parental supervision 15, 53–54; parents bringing inadequate meal 67; practical aspects 53–54; purpose of MFT meals 53; role of MFT team during 54–55; role reversal 90–94; Sunday lunch 88–90; and symptom management 86–94
medical talk 25
mentalization 10–11, 60
MFT (multi-family therapy): apprehension of family members 25; closed groups in 3; development 11; general concepts 13; low drop-out rates 5; meals 53–57; pace 20–21; pre-MFT preparation 34–35; psychological theories influencing 9–11; sharing of knowledge 12; structure 23, *74*; team meetings 12; therapeutic factors *18*; timing 73, *74*
MFT treating team 32–37; ad hoc and unplanned meetings 37; clinical supervision and consultation 37; co-facilitators and helpers 33; content of team meetings 35–36; group coordinator/administrator 33–34; lead facilitators 32–33, 41, 60; members and roles 32–34; pre-group tasks 35; pre-MFT preparation 34–35; role during mealtimes 54–55; team functioning 34; when to meet as a team during MFT 35
MFT-AN (multi-family therapy for anorexia nervosa): for adolescents 3; compared with non-eating disorder-focused family therapy 5; content 27–28; delivery of 3; development 3; early phases 12; and eating disorder focused family therapy 13–17; effectiveness 4–5; evidence for 4; exclusion criteria 7; first day 21; goals of 18; referral for 7; structure 20, 23–27; suitable candidates for 7–8; theoretical concepts 9–17; training 4
mindfulness exercises 111–112
mirrors, one-way 49–50
motivation to recover 6; activities to increase 78–85; challenges 116–120; see-saws 119–120

neurobiology of anorexia nervosa 14–17

1, 2, 3 reveal activity 123–124
one-way mirrors 49–50
overwhelm, feelings of 10

parents: bringing of food to sessions 25, 67; on follow-up activities 121–122; meal supervision 15; meeting up outside group 69; separation and divorce, effect of 7; severe mental health problems 7; validation parent activity 101–102; Where do we stand? activity for 105–106; on workshop activities 80, 92, 94, 97–98, 105, 108, 109
pebble and balloon activity 110
perfectionism 15
personality traits 14
photo cards 78, 111–112
"pleading the fifth amendment" metaphor 24, 25
portraits of anorexia activity 78–80, **81**, **82**, **83**
press conference activity 127–128
pros and cons of anorexia activity 80–83, **84**
psychodrama 12
psychoeducation 13, 14, 15, 55
psychological theories influencing MFT 9–11

Index

randomised controlled trials (RCTs) 3, 5
recovery recipes activity 137, **138**
reflecting teams 49
relationships, exploring impact of illness on, workshop activities 94–101
risk factors for anorexia nervosa: risk management 64–69; temperament and personality traits as 14
role play/role reversal 12, 50, 90–94

self, use of 45
shared goals, setting up 15
siblings 8, 99–101
spaghetti towers activity 115–116
spatial positioning 51
speed dating activity 114–115
starvation, neurological effects 14–17
structure of MFT-AN, four-day intensive workshop 26–27
suitability for MFT-AN 7–8
Sunday lunch activity 88–90

temperament 14
theoretical concepts 3, 9–17; group theories influencing MFT 11–13; psychological theories influencing MFT 9–11; therapeutic alliance 13–14, 61
therapeutic techniques 47–52; connecting families with others 48; connections and differences 48; fishbowls 49–50; interviewing 47; keeping connected 47–48; lived experience and expertise 48–49; mixed family group and "foster families" 50; non-verbal cues, taking account of 48; non-verbal tasks 51; one-way mirrors 49–50; reflecting teams 49; role play/role reversal 50; separate groups 51–52; small group huddle 50–51; spatial positioning 51; subgroups, creating 48
toolboxes activity 108–110
traps and treasures activity 102–106
treatment for anorexia nervosa: acceptability and feasibility 5; broadening of scope 20–21; ending 17; increased intensity 20–21; independent eating, helping to re-establish 16–17; introductory afternoon 23–26; mechanisms of change 5–6; shared goals 15; therapeutic techniques 47–52
troubleshooting: being friendly outside the group 68; competition around eating disorder symptoms arising 68; hostility and defensiveness 67–68; leaving the room 66–67; low attendance at meetings 69; not eating or finishing a meal 67; refusal to speak/take part in activities 65; scenarios 65–69

workshop activities *see* four-day intensive workshop, relevant activities

young people *see* adolescents and young people